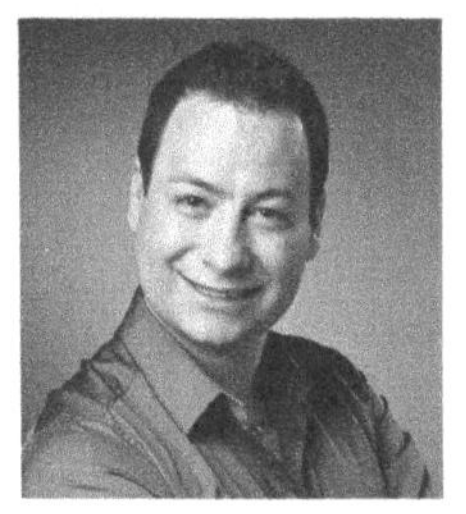

Mitchell Coombes is Australia's most trusted spiritual medium and the best-selling author of *Sensing Spirit: Messages of love, hope and healing from the other side*, *Sensing Psychic: Amazing true stories of everyday psychic encounters*, and *Signs from Spirit: Inspiring true stories from the afterlife*. He is also the creator of the Psychic Soul Oracle Cards.

He writes a weekly advice column in *Woman's Day* and is well known from his countless national radio and television appearances including *Sunrise* and *The Morning Show*.

Mitchell has helped thousands of people worldwide from all walks of life through his extraordinary gift of mediumship, bringing them comfort and transforming lives.

To learn more about his work and schedule, visit Mitchell online at mitchellcoombes.com

SENSING SPIRIT

SENSING SPIRIT

MESSAGES OF HOPE AND HEALING FROM THE OTHER SIDE

MITCHELL COOMBES

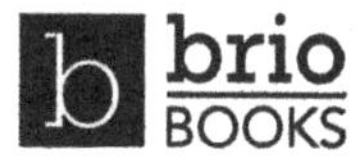

All but a few names have been changed.

First published by Simon & Schuster (Australia) Pty Limited in 2010

Written by Mitchell Coombes with Denise Gibb

ISBN 978-1-922598-72-1 (print)
ISBN 978-1-925143-06-5 (digital)

Published in Australia and New Zealand by:

Brio Books, an imprint of Booktopia Group Ltd
Level 6, 1A Homebush Bay Drive, Rhodes NSW 2138
briobooks.com.au

The paper in this book is FSC® certified. FSC® promotes environmentally responsible, socially beneficial and economically viable management of the world's forests.

Printed and bound in Australia

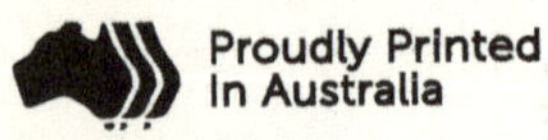

booktopia.com.au

For my grandparents Lino Marano in Heaven
and Lucia Marano on Earth

Contents

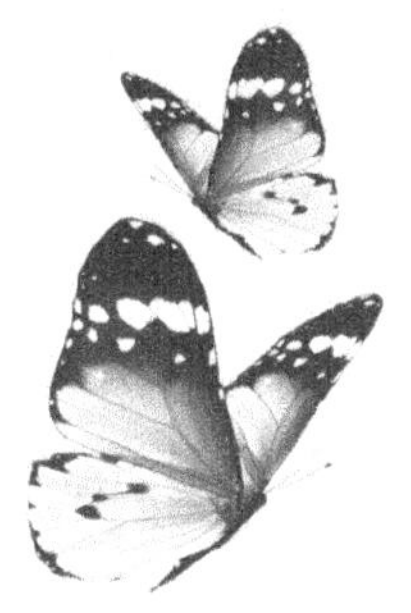

A MESSAGE FROM MITCHELL

Dear Reader,

It's been twelve incredible years since this book first found its way into the hearts and lives of so many. Within these pages are extraordinary true stories of the Spirit World. Stories that offer much hope, healing and reassurance that love really does live forever.

For one reader, Sophie, receiving a heartwarming sign of validation happened after one of my events during a book signing.

At the back of a large auditorium, many people stood in line. As I opened the inside cover of Sophie's book, she said, "I gave this book to mum to read."

She then explained that shortly before her mother passed, her mum handed back the book and said, "Thank you, darling – I now have faith I'll be able to send you a sign after I'm gone."

I was just about to write a special dedication in Sophie's book, when a commotion rippled from the back of the signing line to the front. Suddenly, a solitary bee emerged buzzing around us before landing on the page I was about to write on.

Startled, I put down my pen and looked up at Sophie. Instantly, I saw Sophie's beautiful mum in the Spirit World wrap her arms around Sophie prompting me to ask, "Does this bee mean anything you?"

Sophie nodded, and with tears of joy welling in her eyes, she answered, "Mum was a beekeeper. The day before mum died, she said, 'After I'm gone, I'll send you a bee, so you know it's come from me in Heaven with love'."

As you read the heartwarming stories within the following pages, take comfort that your loved ones in the Spirit World will also draw close to you. After all, they are never too far away. You only need to think of them with love and they will be by your side.

With love, light and many blessings,

— Mitchell Coombes

Australia, April 2022

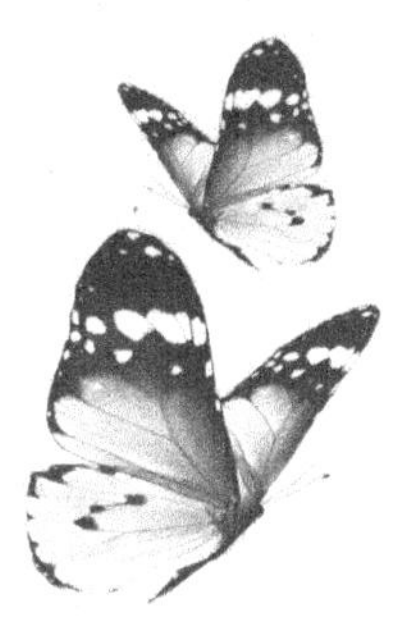

Introduction

What happens when a loved one passes and can they return to visit? What are the signs they send us? What happens when children pass and who looks after them? Where do our pets go? Is there a special place for them too?

When in search of answers to questions like these, many people find themselves seeking the guidance of psychic mediums like me. Over the years, my clientele has included a wide range of fascinating people. I've read for celebrities hoping to make contact with someone special in the Afterlife, mums concerned about the destiny of their children, and high-profile entrepreneurs faced with making multimillion dollar decisions. Rich and famous, business entrepreneur or a fabulous mum at home, I've passed on messages from the Spirit World to people from all walks of life.

It is no coincidence that you are holding *Sensing Spirit* at this very moment – it's the result of divine guidance. Perhaps within these pages you will find the answers to the many questions you've been asking. Maybe you've lost someone you love dearly and have begun questioning your ideas, thoughts, and beliefs. Perhaps you're wondering, 'Is there really life after death?' and, 'Is it possible to be guided from Above?' Or maybe unusual events or happenings have sparked your curiosity.

Have you ever experienced a book falling from its shelf or a newspaper flipping open at a page that gave you the answer to a question you had been grappling with for weeks? Has there been a time when you've been thinking of a departed loved one just as a car passes with a licence plate spelling your loved one's name, initials or date of birth? Perhaps you've suddenly felt the hairs on the back of your neck rise as you've sensed your departed loved one move close to you during a time of great need. If these curious events have happened to you, they are not coincidences; nor are they figments of your imagination – they are special messages sent from Above.

Within the following pages, I share with you remarkable real-life encounters. Encapsulated in each encounter are the words of Spirit that can offer you much hope, healing, guidance, wisdom, encouragement, and inspiration. As you voyage through Sensing Spirit don't be surprised if the experiences of others resonate deep within you, and when they do, take comfort. There is great healing in the discovery that the Spirit World works in the most amazing, wonderful, and life-changing ways.

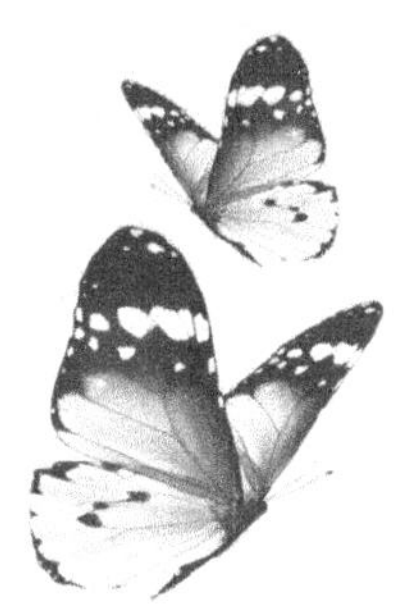

CHAPTER 1

SIXTH SENSE

Just like the little boy in the movie *The Sixth Sense*, I really do see dead people, except as a child I called them 'green people'. I would often wake in the dead of night to find their green human-like forms glowing at the end of my bed. The sight of them petrified me! There were nights when I ran screaming into my parents' room and took refuge in their bed. But with some gentle reassurance from Mum, I slowly began to realise the 'green people' weren't out to hurt me. She said that if I listened they might even speak to me.

When you're born with a gift like mine you assume it is normal. You know no different. So, naturally, I thought everyone could see what I could see. And given I come from a family whose mystical psychic lineage stretches back more than four generations, seeing green people wasn't anything extraordinary in our house.

It wasn't until I started primary school that I realised I was *very* different. I could see things other children could not see. Even the teachers could not see, hear, or feel what I experienced daily.

I constantly received psychic impressions from the people around me – living and passed. As you can imagine, this made me a very sensitive child. So much so that family, friends, and visitors often made comments like, 'Mitchell is certainly an old soul,' 'He's been here before,' and, 'He's been placed on this earth for a very special mission'.

I made my first prediction when I was

three years old. I was outside playing with my favourite toy fire engine. Then, within a flash, my mind fast-forwarded to the next day. To my horror, I saw an army of ants invading Mum's kitchen. So I ran inside to warn her, 'Mum, the ants are coming!' Of course, my bold prediction sounded more like the workings of a creative imagination. Mum raised one eyebrow, questioning me in a loving way. But the next day, my prophecy came true – I was right. Mum woke to discover a huge army of ants swarming all over her kitchen.

One of the most common questions I'm asked is, 'At what age did you become psychic?' The truth is the gift has been with me since birth. I believe we are all born into this world with an important purpose and mission. We each have a destiny to fulfil. Some souls are on this earth to become great actors or artists, to find a cure for an incurable disease, or to bring peace to the world. Others are here to raise beautiful children, to create happy families, and to bring joy to others.

My gift allows me to bring through messages from the Spirit World; a gift for which I am extremely grateful. But what many people do not realise is that psychic mediumship comes with a duty of care. My responsibility is to help others. Therefore, the apprenticeship to Spirit is never an easy one. There are many lessons to learn.

Over the years, life has challenged and tested me. But the good times and the not-so-great ones have helped shape me into the psychic medium I am today.

All life experiences are invaluable – even the tough ones. They present us with the opportunity to learn more about ourselves, others, and the miraculous ways of Spirit.

Today, my 'lessons' have blessed me with an invaluable understanding beyond my years. This understanding places me in a position to empathise with clients and the situations that bring them to me for a reading.

I am so fortunate to have come from a gifted family. My great-great-grandmother Agnes was a visionary gifted with the skill of 'clairvoyance'. She could see the future. Miraculously, one of her premonitions saved her from drowning in quicksand.

My Nanna Lucy is an extremely wise and spiritually gifted woman. She led me to the path that started me on my own spiritual journey. When she was much younger, she was famous for inviting friends over for a 'cuppa' and reading their tea leaves. Everyone would gather around their cups and Nanna would study the patterns the tea leaves had formed. From marriages through to long-awaited pregnancies, Nanna saw it all.

I recall one afternoon when I headed straight from school to Nanna's house. She had just made a fresh brew of tea.

'Come on in and have a cuppa with me,' she called out, before I even got a chance to ring the doorbell.

As we sipped our way through a hot cup of tea, we chatted, laughed, and shared stories about our day. When there was only about half a teaspoon of tea left in my cup, Nanna asked me to hold the cup in my left hand, turn it three times, and hand the cup back to her. When I did, she tipped it upside down on the saucer. After a few seconds, Nanna picked it up again. Bringing it close to her eye, she turned the cup this way and that, carefully studying the various patterns and shapes formed by the leaves. She made me chuckle because it looked like she was viewing the cup through an invisible magnifying glass.

'I can see a U-like symbol in the bottom of your cup, Mitchell,' she announced with a hint of excitement in her voice. 'The U means I can teach you to read tea leaves too.' And so began my first lesson with Nanna learning how to read tea leaves.

Alongside tea-leaf reading, Nanna also taught me how to place a wish out into the universe by using mind power. It didn't take long before the true universal nature of mind power demonstrated itself to me.

Like many children today, I was having an issue with a bully at school. When I told Nanna about it she said, 'Don't get angry. Instead, use the power of your mind in a positive way to make a wish. Ask that something good happens to solve the problem.' So I closed my eyes and wished very hard. Three weeks later the bully was gone – forever. The bully's father – a military man – received an unscheduled transfer. Even the teachers were relieved that day!

My true awakening into the world of Spirit came when Nanna presented me with my first deck of tarot cards. I felt so special because the deck she gave me once belonged to my Uncle Aram – an accomplished astrologer. I still have that deck of cards. I keep them wrapped in a special silk cloth because they are sacred to me.

Learning to read tarot cards ignited my true psychic potential and propelled me into the realm of the truly gifted. However, it didn't happen overnight. When I first began reading tarot cards at the age of twelve, my friends at school would gather around me and ask questions like, 'Will I get married?' 'Will I have kids?' 'Will I be rich?' Each time I would eagerly consult the cards to forecast the outcome.

One Friday afternoon, just after the school bell rang, Natasha rushed up to me and invited me to stay at her house for the weekend. She was planning to invite a few friends over for a 'party'. Before I could answer, I felt a physical tap on my shoulder. When I turned around, no one stood behind me. Yet in that instant, I knew that Natasha's weekend plans spelt trouble. Not wanting to disappoint Natasha, I replied, 'Let's see what the cards reveal.' Within moments of laying out the spread of cards, I sucked in my breath.

'Your mum doesn't know about this party, does she?'

Natasha answered with a sheepish grin.

'Well, she's going to come home early.'

Natasha laughed. She felt sure there was no way her mum would come home early because she was spending the weekend away with her new boyfriend.

'She'll have a huge argument or disagreement and decide to come home early. That's when she busts you,' I added.

The following Monday morning I received my validation. Natasha rushed up to me before first bell.

'Mitchell, you were so right. Mum did come home early. She did bust me.'

'What made her come home early?' I asked.

'She had a big fight with her new boyfriend.'

I recall one time my history teacher surprised my class with a spot test. When I opened the test paper, I panicked. The questions were based on additional reading I hadn't completed. As my eyes glazed over and I stared blankly at the multiple choice answers, I heard a voice say, 'Ask me'. So I did and much to my surprise, then immediate relief, the letter A, B, C, or D appeared in my mind's eye. Can you believe I passed that test with flying colours?

From then on, my tarot cards took a back seat. The dearly departed flooded into all my readings. From deepest fears and sorrows through to favourite colours, Spirit revealed all.

I was so fortunate that my mum understood the mystical ways of Spirit. She encouraged the development of my gift. Just like a coach training an emerging sporting star, Mum taught me self-control, humility, and the rules of spiritual well-being. Mum also imparted wisdom like, 'For the universe to provide you must also have faith it will provide'.

By the time I was fifteen my skill and accuracy had outgrown the short readings I had been giving in the schoolyard at lunchtime. Within me was a burning desire to broaden my psychic horizons and bring through profound messages of healing, love, comfort, and relief to people on a grand scale. The question was, 'How?'

One of Mum's many wisdoms was, 'Trust and leave it in the capable hands of Spirit'. So I did. I sent my wish out into the universe and waited.

Several Sundays later I was walking past my local gift shop. I noticed how quiet the store was. Shoppers were around but they were in and out of other stores, not the gift shop. I heard a voice saying, *If you do readings here the people will find you.* The inspiration hit me like a wall of warm air. I darted inside the shop. I asked the owner if I could set up a card table outside the store and give short readings for *free.* The owner was more than happy to oblige.

Word spread fast. By the second week, the line had doubled. By the third week, it had quadrupled. Eventually, the line of people waiting for their short reading stretched around the corner of the gift shop. My readings were met with comments like, 'Wow, that is amazing,' or, 'How do you see all that in the cards?'

To my surprise, many of the people I did readings for would return with delight saying things like, 'You were bang on the money,' 'Spookily accurate,' and, 'Spot-on'. It was then I realised my skill had gone Beyond. I was truly 'in tune' with Spirit. I knew then I was fulfilling the destiny of my unique soul print.

Don't think for one moment that giving short readings to a huge line of people was easy. It was not. It was terrifying. Rapidly deciphering messages and prophecies from the Spirit World was harder than trying to read fast-scrolling movie credits. The challenge was exhausting. Yet, it felt right. I sensed a higher purpose; I knew there was a reason I needed to master the skill of 'speed-reading' Spirit. So I persisted.

My perseverance paid off. Several years later, the doors to the media world opened. Suddenly I could reach more people. My dream was coming true.

Whenever I am booked to be a guest on a radio or TV show, I'm usually asked, 'How does your gift work?' There are many dimensions to my gift so that question is not easy to answer.

Generally, the Spirit World communicates with me using all my senses. I see, hear, feel, taste, and smell what the Spirit World is trying to communicate. For example, if a departed loved one's passion in life was making strawberry jam I would suddenly *taste* strawberries. Along with that I would most likely *see* a pot of jam simmering on a stovetop. My job as the psychic medium is to piece together all the sensory pieces of information I'm given. In some ways, it's like being given a psychic jigsaw puzzle. Within a very short time, I may be shown signs and symbols, or hear words and phrases from a song, feel pains in my body, see colours, or have visions. Sometimes pieces of information arrive in my dreams the night before! Unlike a real jigsaw puzzle, I don't have the completed picture on the lid of the box to give me clues on where to place the pieces. I have to link all the pieces of psychic information together until they create a clear picture, message, or prediction. The interesting part about that is the psychic pieces of information usually don't go away until I get the picture right. For example, I might sense pain in my chest, suffer from shortness of breath, and feel a pain down my right arm. Quite often I find that what I am feeling, seeing or experiencing will stay with me until I'm able to place the correct interpretation.

Other times Spirit will chat directly into my psychic ear. That can get quite challenging – especially if my client, Spirit, and I are all talking at the same time. One instance that sticks out in my mind is when three ladies came to me for a group reading. As the three ladies sat down a man in spirit stood next to one woman in particular. He was so excited about being there with her he couldn't wait his turn. He just jumped right in and started chatting in my ear – his voice was incredibly clear. 'What?'

I blurted out, startling the three ladies, who had only just managed to get settled in their seats. 'You did *not* go to Paris!'

'Yes I did,' responded one woman, confused.

'No, not you,' I said apologetically, 'I meant your husband. Did you go to Paris *after* he passed?'

'Yes,' she answered.

'Well ... he's here with me now and he says you screamed his name out from the top of the Eiffel Tower. Did you do that?'

'Yes!' she said, overwhelmed by the validation.

'Your husband is telling me he wants you to know he heard you loud and clear. He was standing right by your side,' I explained. 'So it looks like he went to Paris after all.'

Tears of joy filled the woman's eyes. She left her reading elated – her beloved husband was by her side. That's all the validation she needed.

Appearing on television shows such as *The One: The Search for Australia's Most Gifted Psychic* and Channel Seven's *The Morning Show* have brought new dimensions to my psychic gifts. As many of you are probably aware, creating 'good television' means working within technical restraints and time limitations. For instance, throughout a normal reading I occasionally close my eyes. This helps me to fine-tune my focus on Spirit. When appearing on television as a guest, closing your eyes breaks the link the viewer has with you. So I've had to train myself to focus on Spirit with my eyes open.

In the world of television, time will wait for no one – not even the dearly departed. So performing live readings on programs like *The Morning Show* is super challenging. Not only do I have to tune into Spirit with instant clarity, Spirit also must waste no time in making their point. Given I usually have up to three guests to read for within a very short time – sometimes less than seven minutes – Spirit sends me a massive stream of signs, symbols, and messages. That means I have to rapidly sort and select what spirit symbology belongs to whom. That's why I occasionally say, 'I'm not sure if this is for you or you,' and then take a moment to further clarify the information and link the vibration with the correct recipient.

The pressure television places me under to perform rapid short readings with astounding accuracy is the main reason why many psychic mediums prefer not to perform live readings on television or radio. While I admit the pressure is challenging, it does give me immense satisfaction to know I am reaching beyond the one person I'm reading for. Spirit works in the most amazing ways.

Have you ever listened to someone else's reading only to realise that encoded within their reading is a message for you too? After giving live readings on radio and television, I tend to receive many letters and emails from listeners and viewers alike. They write to say thank you and to let me know that the readings I was giving resonated with their own situation – giving them the answers they were seeking.

I find the work of Spirit deeply fulfilling and gratifying. If all I'm able to achieve in this world during this lifetime is to help as many people as I can – then my job is done.

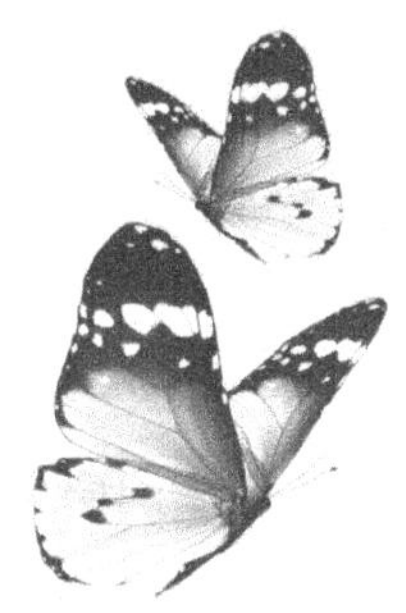

CHAPTER 2

FROM ONE WORLD TO ANOTHER

As Anita slipped into her white nurse's uniform, a sudden pain shot down her left arm. She stopped dressing, took a couple of deep breaths, and waited for the pain to subside. Thinking the pain was nothing more than a strained muscle, Anita continued dressing. After all, she'd spent all morning pulling tough grass roots from her garden beds. She drove to work.

Later that afternoon, Anita placed a blood pressure cuff around the upper arm of one of her six assigned patients. All of a sudden, she felt a sharp shock ricochet through her chest and down her left arm.

'I saw myself fall backwards onto the hard floor. The patient, as sick as he was, leaned over and pressed the cardiac arrest alarm button. I can remember thinking, *He's doing that for me.*

'Lifting out of my body was the most beautiful feeling in the whole world,' Anita explained to me. 'From where I was looking, I could see everywhere at once – even out to my car in the car park – yet I was still hovering above my body.'

The crash cart arrived within seconds. Doctors and nurses crowded around Anita's body, which was lying lifeless on the floor. A young nurse cut open the front of Anita's uniform. Another placed electro pads on her chest. Another connected the wires leading back to the heart monitor. On the screen, a fluorescent green ball drew a flat line. Anita's heart had stopped beating. The doctor and the two nurses were quick to respond as they prepared to defibrillate Anita.

'At that point I drifted out of the room. Somehow, from inside I heard the doctor yell, "Pass the paddles," and then seconds later order, "Stand clear".'

The first shock jolted Anita's body.

'At that point I began racing down a tunnel toward a bright white light. Just before I reached the brightest part of the light, my late husband stepped into view. I felt the most incredible loving feeling. I wanted to hug him, but I couldn't. I didn't have a body. But somehow, he was returning my hug.'

Another shock jolted Anita's body.

'I felt so blessed to see him again. He truly was the love of my life. Then I remembered feeling annoyed that I could hear the unmistakable blip, blip, blip of the heart monitor. I knew what that meant. My late husband smiled and said, "It's not your time. When it is I'll be here waiting for you, but for now, you have to go back."'

His last words to Anita were, 'I love you'.

It's near-death experiences like Anita's that allow the world, not just psychic mediums, to get a glimpse at the greatest mystery of all – death.

Luckily, Anita returned from the brink of death to tell her amazing encounter. But it raises the questions: What really happens when we die? Is death painful? Where do we go? Or is it simply the end?

What happens when we die?

I remember the moment I stopped breathing. I was thirteen. My friend Kiran and I had ventured to the beach early. Overnight, a high tide combined with forceful wave action had washed out sections of the beach leaving unusually high sandy walls. What boy could resist a drop of two metres? So Kiran and I decided to test each other's bravery. Who could stand closest to the edge without it collapsing?

One minute I was standing nearest to the edge looking back at Kiran as if to say, 'I win' – and in the next minute, heavy sand thumped down on my chest, instantly winding me. More sand crashed in on top of me, further compressing my chest and covering my head and body.

Buried alive and no longer able to breathe, I lifted up out of my body. I was in awe. I could see across the ocean and all the way to the horizon. Far below me, Kiran was furiously digging. Even when my heartbeat slowed and my view of the ocean dissolved into a white mist, I was not afraid. I felt calm and at peace. Then a man stepped out from within the mist.

'What are you doing in my dream?' I asked.

'You are not dreaming, Mitchell. This is what it is like to die,' he said.

'But I don't want to die, I'm only thirteen.'

'I know. You and I have work to do back on earth,' he said. 'I am one of your guides.'

At that moment, I heard the scratching of wet sand next to my ear. I was back in my body, but still not breathing. Daylight broke through. I didn't open my eyes. Kiran shuffled closer to me. As he did, he accidently kneed my ribs. The sudden thump followed by sharp pain caused me to suck in a huge breath of air. I sat up, coughed, and freed myself from my sandy grave.

Thanks to Kiran's quick thinking, I didn't pass that day. But for those who do, death occurs when the vital life force leaves and the physical body shuts down. The soul then detaches itself and completely separates from the body. Just as you shed all your clothes before taking a shower, so the soul sheds its body. Those attending the bedside of a dying loved one often sense *that* moment.

'As I cradled Mum's hand and lifted it to my cheek for the very last time I felt an energy stream upwards out of her, and then she was gone,' explained Ellen, a client of mine.

Nurses attending to the dying often report similar experiences.

'It's like the life force whooshes out of the body seconds before all vital organs turn off,' explained Vanessa, a nurse.

Just as no two deaths are the same, not every soul leaves its physical body in the same way. Sometimes a soul will detach from the body and begin its transition well before death arrives.

Just recently, doctors asked a client of mine to consider switching off her husband's life support machine. Only the machine was keeping his heart beating and his lungs breathing. It took two days before my client could bring herself to turn off the switch. Understandably, she suffered feelings of enormous guilt despite the doctor's reassurances she had done the right thing.

Fortunately, I was able to assure my client

her decision was truly a blessing in disguise for her husband. What she had no way of knowing was that his soul had already begun its transition out of the body. By turning off the life support, he was free to complete his journey into the Afterlife. He was eternally grateful to her because his body was no longer anchoring him to the physical world.

While on earth, your body is much like a car. It transports your soul from point A to point B. But unlike your body, your soul does not wear out or deteriorate. If you take the understanding that the soul is energy, science states energy can't be destroyed, it can only ever be transferred. So our souls do go somewhere. That's why I say death is not the end. It simply marks the beginning of a new passage.

Since the 1970s, research into near-death experiences (NDEs) has opened the door on the soul's journey as it heads toward the Afterlife. As you read earlier, I experienced this myself at thirteen when I was trapped under the sand.

But for those who make the full journey, the body goes limp and the vital organs stop functioning. No more air flows in or out of the lungs. The soul enters a blissful void where all pain, illnesses, and afflictions cease. You can still think, remember, see, hear, move, feel, reason, wonder, and question – but you no longer have a physical body. At that point you realise you are still alive, but in a new way.

I recall Sam's experience. While doctors were performing a triple bypass operation on Sam's heart, it suddenly stopped beating.

'I remember looking down on my body on the operating table,' he said. 'I could see myself laying there – my chest cavity open with red and white tubes sprouting out of it everywhere. The doctors and nurse were working hard to revive me, yet I felt so peaceful.'

Within seconds, Sam found himself hurtling down a tunnel at an astonishing speed.

'It made a sort of swishing sound,' he said.

At the end of the tunnel was a bright light.

'I could see one or two people silhouetted in the light. As I drew closer, my grandfather stepped out from within the light. The loving feeling was overwhelming. Replaying through my mind were the wonderful memories I had of the times he spent with me as a child,' he explained. 'I wanted to laugh and cry at the same time, yet he urged me to return to my body.'

The next thing Sam remembered was waking up in the coronary care unit. Only then did he realise he was back in his body and alive.

NDE survivors speak of all sorts of encounters with departed loved ones and friends. Some even speak of conversing with spirit guides as I did. Others report seeing glimpses of their future before returning to their physical body. Either way, NDE experiences mirror the countless images and impressions given to me by Spirit about the Afterlife. So there is no need to be afraid. Death is the liberation of the soul. Death frees the soul so it can be reborn into the nurturing peace and harmony of the Afterlife.

One of the many concerns I hear people express about death is a fear of being alone and lost in a strange new world. Let me reassure you, death is not like driving into a strange city. You're not faced with locating the right address and trying to find somewhere to park on your own. A welcoming party greets every soul entering the Afterlife. And for those who are very young or very ill when they pass, a departed loved one, spirit guide, or loving angel fetches them – as Peta's letter explains.

Dear Mitchell,

You've done readings for me before. I wanted to share this story with you. I'm a paediatric nurse. I have been one for well over ten years now. Not so long ago, I was requested to work a few shifts on the children's oncology ward – the cancer ward. Among my assigned patients was young Patrick, a delightful little five-year-old boy. His leukaemia was not responding well to treatment.

Spying me from a distance Patrick motioned me to come closer. I smiled. I wondered what secret he had to tell. Sick children hospitalised over a long period just love a new face to talk to.

When I stood by his bedside, Patrick patted it as if to say sit down. So I did.

'The angel will come for me tonight,' he whispered in my ear.

I was shocked, but played along.

'What makes you think that?' I whispered.

'He told me and Teddy last night,' said Patrick, holding his teddy bear up to my face and smiling.

It wasn't the first time I had nursed dying children. So I didn't laugh off his 'angel' encounter.

'What else did the angel say?' I asked.

'Mummy and Daddy will see me again in Heaven.'

The next morning, I arrived half an hour early for my shift and headed straight to Patrick's room. His bed was empty. My heart sank. The night-duty nurse looked at me with tears in her eyes.

'When?' I asked.

'Three o'clock this morning,' she replied.

Peta's sad but heartwarming story is like many others I've heard where a departed loved one or angel has visited to reassure the one about to pass that they will not be alone in their passage to the Afterlife.

Very young or very old, the arrival of any soul in the Afterlife is a joyous reunion. Much like the birth of a long-awaited grandchild, departed loved ones and spiritual guides gather with much excitement and joy.

For the many of you who have nursed a dying loved one, you're left with the memory of the last moment fresh in your mind. This is not so bad if your loved one passed peacefully. Many don't. But let me give you some peace of mind. Departed loved ones enter the Afterlife with all memories, personality traits, and intelligence intact. They have a concept of who they were before they died. But all physical disabilities, illnesses, addictions, or pains are shed along with the body. So try not to remember images of your loved one in their final moment. Instead, remember them when they were fit and healthy because that's how they remember themselves.

When I connect with departed loved ones, they show images of themselves at their best – the things you remember them for most. Tall, blue eyes with an infectious laugh; walked with a limp, or liked to collect buttons. If a loved one wants to show me how they passed, I might see the flash of a cigarette packet and feel tightness in my chest. When that happens, I know they had something wrong in the lung or chest region.

Fortunately, when I see and feel these things it is *not* how your departed loved one is feeling in the Afterlife. These feelings and images serve only as points of validation. That way I know I am connecting the right dearly departed with the right person.

Sometimes it is not so easy to establish a strong connection with a newly passed soul. Some even say the soul lingers for three, seven, or eleven days before finally making a full transition into the Afterlife – as Lynette's story suggests.

After Lynette's mother's cremation, mourners started arriving at the house. Lynette was inconsolable. So her sister, Natalie, took Lynette by the hand and led her out into their mother's garden.

'She's not in the house. I can feel her energy in the garden,' Natalie recalled telling her sister.

Lynette broke down and cried even harder

when Natalie asked her to stop in front of a glorious pink and white camellia bush. Once Lynette's tears eased, she managed to say, 'This is exactly where Mum and I would sit every Tuesday and enjoy a cup of tea.'

Two weeks later, when Natalie visited the pink and white camellia bush on her own, she could no longer feel her mother's soul. She took comfort knowing her mum's journey into the Afterlife was well underway.

No two souls make their transition into the Afterlife the same way. I sense it very much depends on the circumstances surrounding the soul's passing and the needs of grieving loved ones left behind.

The soul's journey

Under normal circumstances, the soul's transition into the Afterlife is rapid. Once the joyous reunion with departed loved ones and spirit guides is over, the soul can look forward to many glorious days of learning and developing spiritually. The Afterlife is a positive, peaceful, and loving place full of opportunities. However, if a soul's passing was sudden, accidental, or unexpected, the transition may take a little longer.

Do you remember Malcolm Crowe, the child psychologist in the movie *The Sixth Sense*? It takes time for him to realise *he* is the one who is dead – thanks to a small boy who can see dead people. Like Malcolm, those who die suddenly, accidentally or unexpectedly can take a little longer to work it out.

Sometimes, the loved one living needs time to adjust when the passing of a loved one has been sudden, accidental, or unexpected.

Tony was well into his seventies. I first met him seated at an alfresco café. Such a cloud of sadness hung over him I stopped in my tracks. I just wanted to cry. I was about to continue walking when a kind loving woman came through in spirit.

'Tell him I understand why he wasn't there,' she communicated.

I knew then I was looking at a man who had lost the love of his life.

Rarely do I approach strangers in the street with a message from a departed loved one. But in Tony's case, I made an exception. 'You look like you could do with some company,' I said, pulling out a chair and sitting opposite Tony. He made no protest at my intrusion. Two weeks ago, one phone call turned Tony's life upside down.

'Your brother has gone into renal failure. He's asking for you,' said the nurse on the other end of the phone.

Tony knew he needed to drop everything and drive to the city, but he couldn't. At home, he was nursing Irene, his sick wife. Not sure what to do, Tony rang his doctor. The doctor suggested he admit Irene to the local hospital for 24-hour respite care. A neighbour offered to tend to his cattle.

Tony arrived at the city hospital just twenty minutes too late. His brother had already passed away. Tony was too shocked to cry. Hours later, he found himself driving home, confused and angry. *People don't die from leg ulcers. Surely, they could have saved him?* Tony kept repeating to himself.

With the first signs of driver fatigue setting in, Tony decided to make an unscheduled stop. One of his farming friends lived halfway between the city and home. His friends welcomed him warmly and then later comforted him once they understood his ordeal. Meanwhile, back at home, his phone was constantly ringing.

Next morning, Tony rose early and set off home. It was still dark when he arrived at the hospital to collect Irene.

'When I walked in the room where I left Irene, her bed was empty,' said Tony, as tears filled his eyes. 'A nurse rushed in behind me, saying, "We tried to call you."'

Naturally, Tony thought the nurse was going to tell him Irene was relocated to another room – as so often happens in hospitals. 'I'm so sorry,' said the nurse, 'Irene passed away two hours ago.'

'Was Irene a petite pretty woman with dark hair and green eyes?' I asked.

Tony just nodded. I could feel his overwhelming sadness.

'Was her pet name for you bunnikins?'

Tony stiffened. That's when I explained I was a psychic medium. 'Tony, Irene understands. She knows why you were not by her side in her final hour. She doesn't want you to feel guilty any more.'

Irene explained she would have passed earlier, but Tony's need and love for her was so great, he kept her earthbound. Her soul was not free to leave.

Given my many encounters with spirits, I've come to understand that there is a small degree of choice as to *when* a soul leaves its body. Many of my clients are nurses. Amy said to me one day, 'It's amazing the number of souls that pass minutes after family leave the room to take a short break.'

No one ever dies alone. I reassured Tony that Irene did not die alone. Her loving departed mother came to fetch her, saying, 'You can go now.' So what might appear as a lonely passing in the physical world is not. A loving relative, departed parent, guardian angel, or spirit guide is always waiting to collect and guide a loved one crossing over to the Afterlife.

Arriving in the Afterlife marks the completion of an earthly life cycle and the start of a new one in the Afterlife. But what happens if a soul does not fulfil its earthly life cycle? What happens if a person dies before his or her time?

Passing before time

Aiden was just seventeen when he jumped off a cliff. An unsuspecting fisherman found his body lying cold and lifeless on the rocks. One of the two police officers attending the scene identified Aiden immediately. He'd come to know Aiden and his mother, Eva, as a result of Aiden's drug addiction problems. Saddened, he covered Aiden's body and knelt by his side. How was he going to break the news to Aiden's mother? Aiden appeared to be going so well. He was attending a drug rehabilitation program and had been clean for months. What went wrong?

That question, 'Why did Aiden take his own life?' is what brought Eva to me ten months later. She could not find closure or peace.

'I did everything right,' she explained to me. 'He was slipping into depression, so I took him straight to the doctor. The doctor gave him antidepressants.'

When I connected with Aiden, the first thing he said was, 'Tell Mum I'm sorry.'

Despite the methadone program, Aiden was struggling. At times, the physical pain was too much and the addictive urges sent him into blind rages – most of which he directed at his mum. But the worst part was saying, 'No,' to his friends.

Aiden communicated that he felt torn. He wanted to get off the drugs but he didn't want to lose his friends. In the end, he thought it would be easier to take his own life.

I think we've all had times where we haven't been able to see our way clear of a problem. I felt deeply for Aiden's mum, Eva. Here was a mother who had given birth to a beautiful baby boy; a mother who had worked hard to feed, clothe and educate her son; a mother who picked her son up when he fell, patched his scrapped knees, and taught him how to stand up for himself in a very tough world. Sadly, it wasn't until Aiden had crossed over that he realised he'd repaid his mum's unconditional love by giving up on himself.

Some religions teach that the soul of a person who takes their own life will never gain entry into the Afterlife. I've been asked so many times, 'Will my son go to hell?' 'Will my daughter's soul be lost in all eternity?' Please understand the Afterlife is non-judgmental. *All* souls enter the Afterlife. Have no fear about that. Entry into the Afterlife is unconditional, as is the love, support, and comfort given there.

Transitional healing

Sadly, Aiden's life ended before his time and certainly not in accordance with his unique soul print.

Like all souls, Aiden was welcomed into the Afterlife and surrounded by unconditional love. But I sense that thereafter Aiden went straight to a special level within the Spirit World. There he received intensive tuition.

'I thought I'd taken the easy way out,' Aiden communicated during the reading. 'But now I realise I have a lot of hard work to do to make up for what I did.'

Aiden shared with me flashes of images – almost like a movie of his life. Most souls who suicide show me something similar. I sense Aiden was taken through a life review. From birth through to the moment he passed, specialised guides and angels set about helping Aiden learn from his mistakes in a loving and non-judgmental way. Once souls like Aiden learn from their mistakes, a monumental shift takes place in their spiritual healing and development.

For loved ones left in the wake of a suicide, like Aiden's mum, they often have confused and painful emotions. Worst of all is the sense of guilt, shame, and failure. 'Could I have prevented it?' 'I should have seen it coming.' 'If only we hadn't had a fight that night.' Fortunately, I was able to reassure Eva that Aiden was in the hands of divine healers within the Spirit World. Although he was no longer with her in the physical world, he would always be with her in spirit. Finally, Eva was able to find closure and begin her journey.

Murder – the taking of a life

Bella, a client of mine, came close to stepping off her emotional edge after receiving a phone call from police in Greece.

'What do you mean he is dead?' exclaimed Bella, instantly numb.

Bella's son Nathan was working his way around Europe. She had spoken to him two days earlier. He was working as a barman in a nightclub in Greece. He'd made friends and was excited that they'd invited him to a party that night.

What Nathan didn't realise was that his 'friends' had strong underworld connections.

The morning after the party, a gardener found Nathan, dead. The Greek police were harsh. Nathan was just another drunk foreigner who fell to his death. Even more distressing, when Bella arrived in Greece with her husband, the evidence did not add up – even to a novice like her. And no one seemed concerned that

Nathan's passport was missing, as were his personal effects.

Unsatisfied, Bella braved viewing her son's body in the mortuary. Bruising on his wrists suggested he'd been restrained. All of which just added to the many unanswered questions that troubled her. Yet, there was one thing Bella was sure of – her son did not jump or fall from a balcony. He was pushed. Nathan was murdered.

Losing a loved one to murder, or to any other horrific crime, is one of the worst pains the human heart can endure. The loss is overwhelming; the sense of despair and hopelessness unbearable.

Tapping into the spirit of a murder victim can be emotionally distressing for the client and me. This is because I don't hold back information. I tell it as Spirit shares it. So I see firsthand flashes of the murder or I sense through my own body how the victim died. As distressing as it may be, Spirit helps me find the missing clues or the answers to hard questions like, 'Did my loved one suffer?' 'Will my loved one ever find peace?'

Even though the Greek police ruled Nathan's death was a closed case, Bella could not find closure. That's why she came to me.

I will only investigate murder or missing person's cases at the request of the grieving family. I know there have been many instances where mediums have collectively investigated a cold case. For me, the family's consent and cooperation are most important. Their love and karmic bond are essential if I am to make a strong connection with the victim that gets results. The information given to me may not always solve the crime. However, what I do find is that the information given to me is usually what the family needs to bring about closure.

In Bella's case, Nathan communicated to me that he did not feel his body hit the ground. Just before the point of impact, he floated above the scene, aware of what was happening but free from any associated pain. He was sad to leave his mum and friends, but quickly realised something greater awaited him.

Souls that pass traumatically, like Nathan, receive specialised care from spirit guides and angels in a spirit hospital before progressing forward to the Spirit World.

In some cases, murder victims delay making a complete transition into the Afterlife. They remain earthbound.

Souls can remain earthbound for a number of different reasons. Murder victims, like Nathan, for example, often choose to remain earthbound until family members learn of their passing or until missing clues are found.

Curiously, paranormal activity in some murder cases links directly to the departed loved one trying to communicate the circumstances of their passing to a loved one living. On rare occasions, the soul of a murder victim may need a soul retrieval expert to step in and help before it can continue into the Afterlife.

Thankfully, earthbound souls transcend rapidly once their message is understood.

You may not realise it but emotional healing and recovering from a traumatic loss is a two-way connection. A soul's progress in the Afterlife often synchronises with their loved ones' grieving process in the physical world. That's why prayers of love, light and healing sent to loved ones are so important.

Souls offline

In the past, I've helped many clients create a daily grief ritual – such as lighting a candle and sending healing and loving thoughts into the Afterlife. No deed or prayer goes unheard or without effect. Several times clients have come back to me and said, 'No matter how much I pray, my loved one won't give me a sign he or she is in Heaven.'

Callie came to me for a reading within two days of her mother passing. Try as I did, I could not connect with Callie's mother. Instead, I connected with a grandmother Callie had never met. She told me Callie's mum was offline.

Rarely are souls offline to the physical world, but when they are it is usually because they are very new in spirit or they're on higher spiritual duties. I feel for my clients on the rare occasions this happens. Should that ever happen to you in a reading, I ask you to think of it this way. If you're totally absorbed cooking up a storm in the kitchen while your husband is at work, and your older kids are at school and the baby is asleep, does it mean you don't care about them? Of course not. It just means you're occupied with another task at that point in time, just as your husband, kids and baby are. So is the case in the Afterlife. When your departed loved ones are offline, they are busy with higher duties. Even though they can't answer you immediately, you're never out of their thoughts.

Souls that kiss the earth

One, two, three, four, five, six, seven, all good children go to Heaven. Do you remember this rhyme? I do. Mum taught it to me when I was little. But for all its heavenly wisdom, it's not quite true. All children go to Heaven, not just the good ones.

It seems wrong when a little one or child passes. How can it be that their soul only kisses the earth for such a short time before it leaves again? It hardly seems fair that some children arrive in the physical world with a very short karmic path.

One night I was up late. In front of me was a pile of emails and letters given to me by the editor of *That's Life* magazine. Choosing one is difficult, but before I do I gather all the letters together and spend time in prayer and meditation. I ask the dearly departed belonging to those who have written to send their loved ones a sign that answers their question. I then ask my own spirit guides to help me choose one letter to answer.

After reading about three quarters of the letters and emails, I was fighting to keep my eyes open. I was about to put the remaining few letters aside when a small boy – about seven or eight years old – connected with me. (I later found out his name was Tommy.)

'You can't stop now,' he said. 'You haven't read my grandma's letter.'

With that Tommy created a slight draught. It scattered the remaining letters. One letter landed face-up on my coffee table directly in front of me. The rest landed on the floor near my feet. The letter read:

Dear Mitchell,

Are you able to connect with my grandson Tommy?

That was it; short and simple.

'Daddy blames himself,' said Tommy, not

letting our connection go.

So I held the letter, closed my eyes, and concentrated on strengthening my connection with Tommy.

As in life, Tommy was a chatterbox. There was no need to prompt him. He had spirit communication mastered.

'Daddy blames himself,' he repeated. The next image Tommy flashed through my mind made me gasp with horror.

'I want Daddy to be happy again,' he said.

Tommy's dad drove trucks for a living. Every school morning Tommy would ride up in the front of the truck with his dad. His dad would drop him off at the school gate. One morning Tommy jumped out of the truck. Tommy's dad drove off as normal. He had no idea that Tommy had somehow slipped or fallen under the truck. No one knows how but Tommy's dad accidentally ran over Tommy, killing him instantly.

There is no misery greater than losing a

child. And even though I know that for every child that passes an angel is born, it brings little comfort at the time.

Every child-loss story is different in its own sad way. Parents come to me and ask questions like, 'Pete was just four years old. He was too young to know anyone in Heaven. Who will care for him now?' Or 'Will my Jessie have warm clothes in Heaven?'

If you've lost a little one, know that children transcend with all memories, personality traits, and intelligence intact. Any pain suffered along with any physical disability or illness stays behind with the body.

A departed loved one or angel often fetches very young children. But always, departed grandparents, spirit guides, angels, or even pets are there to greet the child into the Afterlife. But that is just the beginning. From the glimpses I've been given by my spirit guides, children enter a magical world especially designed for them.

I've been shown nurseries where angels devote their time to the loving care and spiritual development of babies and toddlers. Slightly older children go to spirit school where they take part in fun activities.

When I connect with spirit children, I'm given a picture of key physical characteristics and personality traits that identify the child at the time of his or her passing. But sometimes, I connect with spirit children for the first time some twenty years after. When that happens I'm shown who they were as a child in the physical world but also who they are as an adult in the Spirit World.

I first encountered Logan in spirit through his mother, Ava. Logan lost his battle with cystic fibrosis at the age of twelve. It brought tears of joy to Ava when I said, 'Logan is presenting to me as a young man in motorcross bike-riding gear.'

'Logan's dream was to become a motorcross champion,' said Ava.

'He wants you to know that had he survived he would have been just that, but know he's guiding and protecting children with the same dream.'

All children continue to grow and learn in spirit. Some may even move on to become spirit guides and help others.

Perhaps the most heartwarming of all is when I connect with spirit children who demonstrate just how much they are still a part of their parents' life in the living world – even years after passing.

Sophie's youngest son, Zac, passed due to a terrible accident. He climbed out of the bath, lost his footing on the wet tiles, slipped, and hit his head. He made no sound. Sophie only discovered the tragic accident when she went to check on him. She immediately rendered first aid and called for an ambulance. But unfortunately, Zac didn't pull through. He passed due to a severe head injury.

Five years on, Sophie sat in front of me,

expecting. With three weeks to go, she was excited about the birth of her new baby.

Zac came through with just as much excitement about his new 'brother'. Even Sophie didn't know the sex of her baby at that stage. I kept that from her. I didn't want to spoil her joy.

'Tell Mum it's okay to give the baby the remote control car when he's old enough,' communicated Zac. I passed on the message, careful to be non-gender specific. Sophie looked at me dumbfounded.

'How did he know? He died before his birthday – before I could give it to him.'

'Zac is around you and still very much a part of your family,' I explained.

Sophie also felt very guilty for converting Zac's room into a nursery.

'I hope Zac doesn't think we're trying to replace him?' she confessed to me. Zac responded with, 'Tell Mum I'm so glad she chose my room for the new nursery. The new baby will love it.'

Just like spirit children, babies too can connect and offer great comfort as Zac did. Usually a departed family member or someone lovingly bonded to the family in some way will bring the child through.

Sometimes, when I make contact with a departed loved one I find a spirit baby with them – one that did not make it to the physical world. When this happens, I know the person I'm reading for has suffered the loss of a very little one as a result of a stillbirth, miscarriage, or termination.

Spirit has shown me that unborn souls who don't arrive in the physical world, for whatever reason, are sent back to a special nursery. Once there, angels and spirit guides nurture them with tender loving care. Some go on and choose another karmic path. Others remain in spirit continuing to grow so they can eventually guide others.

While I am very respectful of different religious and cultural beliefs concerning stillbirths, miscarriages and terminations, Spirit has shown me it is non-judgmental.

Departed loved ones don't bring unborn souls forward to chastise or punish. Instead, they bring them through to comfort the mother; to ease her feeling of guilt or shame. The Spirit World understands why a termination or miscarriage occurred. No judgment takes place. Spirit is simply reassuring the mother that the soul of her unborn baby continues to grow and live on in the Afterlife.

If you've lost a little one, or know someone who has, I can reassure you babies, toddlers, and children maintain a spiritual bond with their earthly parents and family. They'll be with you in spirit for the rest of your natural life. So talk to them. Send all your loving thoughts and prayers. Every one of them will help your little one grow and learn in spirit.

The Afterlife is a glorious world filled with opportunity for all souls. At times, the Afterlife bustles with intense activity, learning, and development. Other times it's a paradise of heavenly peace and rest.

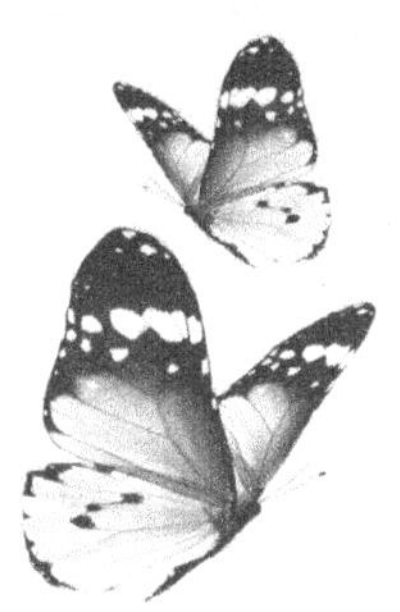

CHAPTER 3

SPIRIT WORLD

Every day, I communicate messages of comfort, love, healing, and advice on behalf of the Spirit World. For me, every message given by a departed loved one is a validation that our souls do go somewhere after we pass. Some people refer to that 'somewhere' as Heaven, while others think of it as the Spirit World, Nirvana, or the Afterlife. To me the name is not as important as the understanding. So feel free to substitute your preferred name for the Afterlife while you're reading.

Over the years, Spirit has shown me glimpses of what the Afterlife may present. I can tell you that the Afterlife – or Spirit World – is not a three-dimensional place with a geographical location. While you'll never find it on a map, it is much closer than many realise.

The Spirit World does not abound with fluffy white clouds or rage like a fiery furnace of flames. There is no Heaven above or Hell below us. The Spirit World is a continuum in which souls evolve toward their optimum level of purity.

Two years ago, a young woman named Chloe arrived at my rooms for a reading. During the course of her reading, I sensed she had an overwhelming fear of dying.

It was then Chloe told me she was on tenterhooks. Up until recently, Chloe regularly visited a tanning solarium. Then one morning she felt a sore spot on her back. When she looked in the mirror, the sore spot on her back was a raised and angry-looking mole. Her doctor performed an immediate biopsy and sent the sample away for urgent testing. He suspected the mole had turned cancerous. Chloe feared it was a melanoma and was praying for her life. 'I've done things to hurt the people I love,' confessed Chloe. 'Just in case – I've even asked God not to punish me and allow me into Heaven.'

Like many people I have read for over the years, Chloe's fears came from a mix of her religious beliefs and family and cultural conditioning. I explained to Chloe that *everyone* gains entry into the Afterlife. She had no need to worry about that. I also reassured Chloe she would be lucky this time. Spirit was telling me she did not have skin cancer. She had many more years to live. However, Chloe's narrow escape with death was a blessing in disguise. Her cancer scare presented her with the opportunity to change her ways and make amends, *if* she chose to. Just like with Chloe, the Spirit World also presents each soul with opportunities to evolve and grow spiritually.

Although the Spirit World does not have a geographical location, it consists of many realms. Within each realm are levels of spiritual being. When departed loved ones first arrive in the Spirit World, their souls gravitate to a level that best reflects the way they lived their human lives. Thereafter, souls continue to grow and advance to new levels until they reach their optimal level of purity.

Do you recall Aiden from the previous chapter? Sadly, Aiden committed suicide. I sense he gravitated to a level best suited to helping suicide victims. And Zac – the little boy who tragically passed after slipping over in the bathroom – I sense he gravitated toward a level best suited for his needs.

In one way, levels within the Spirit World are like classrooms. Each level specialises in a specific subject. But unlike a four-walled classroom on earth, souls are not confined. They can move freely between the spirit realms and the physical world.

Readers of my column in *That's Life* magazine often write and ask what happens to the souls of people who commit murder, rape or other heinous crimes. My answer is – those souls 'do time' on a level that accurately reflects the way they lived their human lives. They are monitored closely and are subject to intensive instruction until they begin to advance spiritually.

Another popular question is, 'Do we age in the Spirit World?' The curious thing about the Spirit World is that it cannot be measured by what we know and understand in the physical world. Time, dimension, and space have no relevance. So in answer to that question, souls do not age in a physical sense. Instead, they advance toward spiritual maturity.

At the age of six, Dianne's beautiful boy Stevie was something of a child prodigy. His talent as a pianist was astounding. Three months before his seventh birthday, Dianne heard Stevie screaming. Dianne ran to the scene to find Stevie clutching a broken left forearm. Stevie's older brother was sobbing with remorse, 'All I did was grab his arm, Mum. I didn't mean to hurt Stevie.'

Stevie was crying too, but not from the pain as you would expect.

'I'll never play again,' he sobbed.

Dianne reassured Stevie his arm would soon mend and he would be playing the piano again in next to no time. Sadly, Stevie was right. A routine X-ray of his broken arm revealed a rare form of incurable bone cancer. Stevie died several months later.

I first met Dianne on the tenth anniversary of Stevie's passing. She came to me for a reading, hoping to connect with her young son in spirit. You can imagine Dianne's surprise then flood of tears when I said, 'I have a young man in spirit. He's wearing a black tail coat and seated at a grand piano. He is playing the most beautiful music.'

By showing himself as a young man in

his early twenties Stevie was giving me two messages. First, he was reassuring his much-loved mum that he was living his dream in the Afterlife. Second, he was helping me to understand his soul had grown spiritually.

Just as there is no measurement for time in the Afterlife, distance too cannot be measured. Consequently, there is no need for buses, trains, planes, or cars in the Spirit World. Travel is by thought. Departure to and arrival at a destination is instant. If departed loved ones wish to be by your side they are in an instant. How fortunate travel is so easy. Our departed loved ones are frequent visitors because they love and miss us as much as we do them.

Have you ever wondered what it is like to be a soul living in the Spirit World? Many people do. I sense it is similar to the experience we have when we dream. During sleep, our physical body is at rest. Our mind is free to travel and enter other levels of consciousness. During our dreams we feel the same and people we know recognise us. We have adventures and our emotions feel real – as do physical sensations like flying, running up a hill or lying on a sandy beach. Yet this all happens in our dreams without our physical body. I sense being in spirit is a similar experience.

Angels and spirit guides

Angels and spirit guides reside in the Afterlife along with our departed loved ones. Before we are born, a guardian angel and several spirit guides are assigned to us. Their purpose is to guide and protect us as we journey through our physical life experience. Our guides are responsible for delivering timely messages, healing remedies, and in some cases, intervening with life-saving measures. For that reason, I like to think of our guides as teachers assigned to help us while we're in earth's classroom.

As our needs and circumstances change throughout life, so do our guides. This is such a blessing. It means the best-qualified guide steps forward to help. Imagine if Albert Einstein's only guide was best qualified in matters of art and Claude Monet's guide was best qualified in matters of science. Would Albert Einstein have discovered the theory of relativity? Would Claude Monet have painted his famous *Water Lily Pond*? Maybe not.

One guide, above all others, is responsible for coordinating all our guardian angel's requests, guides, and spirit helpers. He or she holds the master plan to our life – our soul print. Our master guide ensures all the elements we need to fulfil our destiny fall into place at the right time.

I, for example, have a guide who steps forward to help me with my readings. For years, I was curious as to his identity and kept asking for clues. Then over the course of eight weeks, four red feathers appeared out of nowhere. I found the first red feather lying on the mat outside my front door at midnight, the second red feather was wedged into my letterbox on a Sunday and the third red feather floated down from the sky above me – in a supermarket car park of all places. When the fourth red feather washed up around my ankles at the beach, I realised Spirit was trying to give me a message. The question was *who* and *what* was the message. So I began meditating to find out.

Several nights later, during a dream, the outline of a human figure partially formed in front of me. I heard a man's voice say, 'Red Feather'. Suddenly, my body jolted and I woke sitting upright in bed. I realised then that 'Red Feather' was the name of my spirit guide. Naturally, I asked again if I could see Red Feather.

Not long after that dream, I was deep in meditation. I was asking Red Feather to reveal his identity. While floating in a peaceful void the image of a red feather formed in my mind's eye. I felt sure Red Feather would show, but he did not.

For months I meditated, asking Red Feather to reveal his identity, but nothing happened. So I switched tack and asked him to appear in my dreams. After all, dreams are wonderful portals to the Spirit World. Each morning I woke disappointed. Then one morning I woke to hear the words, 'Expectations block Spirit'. I understood immediately. I had to 'let go' of all my expectations concerning Red Feather.

Not long afterwards, I had just stepped off stage after presenting a very successful seminar. I felt a tap on my shoulder. I turned around. A woman stood in front of me smiling.

'I don't normally do this,' she said, 'but I was in the audience and Spirit told me that *this* is for you!'

The woman promptly handed me an envelope.

'But before you open it, I have to tell you red feathers are important,' she said.

Within the envelope sat an A4-sized piece of art paper. As I slid the paper out of the envelope, the eyes of an American Indian met mine. The woman's skill as a spiritual artist was immediately evident. The Indian's face appeared warm, rich, and alive with detail. He was wearing a chief's headdress. Four red feathers stood out from the rest. I was speechless. They were the exact same four red feathers I had collected. *Red Feather*, I thought. *So that's what you look like.*

Your guides want you to feel comfortable and at ease with them. When the student is ready, the teacher will appear.

One client of mine knows her guide as a Tibetan monk, another says her guide is a goddess from Atlantis and another says his is from the Lemurian ruins. It's a glorious moment when your spirit guides reveal their identity, but I have to say some people place too much importance on identifying their guides. You don't have to know who your guides are or where they're from before you ask for their help.

Think back to what happens when you meet someone for the very first time who is now a close friend. How many conversations did it take before you uncovered personal details about where they worked, where they lived and who their family members were? Personally, I believe true friendships strengthen and deepen over time. Getting to know guides is no different to fostering a new friendship. So take the pressure off yourself. Talk to your guides often. Ask them to help you in all aspects of your life. Let your friendship unfold and develop naturally – as I eventually did with Red Feather. Believe me, your guides will make every attempt to communicate with you. And over time, you'll discover their answers will arrive in any number of forms including dreams, signs, feelings, symbols, and even animal messengers.

Your unique soul print

Many people, belief systems, and cultures throughout the world believe that our souls choose the life we live and the lessons we need to learn *before* we are born. That is why I say *nothing* in our lives happens by chance. Our lives are not a series of random or haphazard events. There *is* a divine plan in place that guides each one of us. I call this plan the *soul print.*

Evidence of a soul print exists in many aspects of our lives. Have you heard the expression, 'You hold the future in the palm of your hands'? Well, it's true. I sense the lines on the palm of our hands are a miniature carbon copy of our soul print. Encoded within the lines on our hands are elements of our past life, present life, and future. Although I don't use palmistry to obtain a client's soul print information, those who do give amazingly accurate readings.

Not so long ago Reannon came to me for

a reading. When I asked if I could hold a piece of her jewellery she slipped off her wedding ring, handed it to me and said, 'He left me six months ago.'

Reannon's apparent ease with her recent separation stirred my curiosity.

When I connected with Spirit, I was shown elements of Reannon's soul print that revealed glimpses of her past, present and future. 'Despite your heartache, I sense your husband has been a blessing,' I said. 'You've made so many changes since you separated.'

'You're so right, Mitchell. I have emerged a new woman. I've discovered a strength and a confidence I never knew I had,' said Reannon.

As the reading continued, I looked further into Reannon's future. Within her soul print was another man – one that would sweep her off her feet.

'There is a man with a J sounding name about to come into your life. He'll have dark hair, dark brown eyes, drive a red car and work with his hands for a living. What's more, you'll have a baby with this man.'

At that moment, I saw a flash of pink and added, 'It will be a girl.'

One year later, Reannon sat in front of me bursting with excitement.

'Mitchell, the man you described *did* walk into my life. He has dark hair, beautiful brown eyes, drives a fabulous red car and his name is Jay – just like you said.'

Incredibly, Reannon later revealed Jay too had visited a psychic long before meeting her. That psychic, they eventually realised, was none other than me! Back then, I could see in Jay's soul print that he would meet and fall in love with a beautiful woman. The woman I described to Jay was, of course, Reannon.

On face value, the odds of Reannon and Jay meeting were stacked against them. Reannon lived in northern New South Wales and Jay lived near the southern border, yet it was within both of their destinities to meet.

Reannon and Jay were a part of each other's soul print. Their paths were meant to cross. They were destined to foster a relationship and create a loving future together. I'm delighted to report during the writing of this chapter I received word that Reannon and Jay became proud parents of a beautiful baby girl – just like I said. How wonderful is that?

Reannon's story demonstrates that divine forces are always at work to ensure we follow our unique soul print. For that reason, I like to think of our soul print as a map. The map starts at our birth and progresses forward until it ends at our ultimate destination – our passing and return home to the Spirit World. Just like a map, all the landmarks, towns, roads, streets, rivers, and hills that intersect our personal road represent the *major* events in our life. One person's road may lead them toward raising wonderful children. Meanwhile, the life highway someone else is following may lead him or her toward inventing a cure for an incurable disease, or creating great works of literature, art, or music. For others their road may end only after passing through a few towns. All of us are born with a definite road to follow and a unique purpose to fulfil. And for those of you who have grieved over a decision to terminate a pregnancy, or have lost a little one to a miscarriage or stillbirth, take heart. Your little ones knew they did not have far to travel. Take comfort – it was part of their plan too.

Outside of the major events mapped on our soul print, we are free to choose the roads we travel. We have free will. Life is up to us.

Bill came to me for a general psychic reading. He was considering buying a business. Looking into his soul print, I saw the symbol for bankruptcy and the number two.

'Spirit is showing me you'll be bankrupt within two years,' I said.

Of course, that was not what Bill wanted to hear. He asked me to double-check. I did. Spirit still gave me the same answer. Nevertheless,

Bill had made up his mind. He was going to buy the business. That was his choice.

Three years later, Bill booked in for another reading.

'You were wrong,' he said, 'I went bankrupt after three years.' Bankrupt within two or three years was not the point. Running a successful business was not a part of Bill's destiny. It was not in his soul print.

Even though we exercise our free will we cannot change or avoid major events mapped within our soul print. Reannon, for example, was destined to meet Jay irrespective of how far apart they lived at the time. They were destined to raise a beautiful baby girl. Bill, on the other hand, was destined not to win in business – he was destined to succeed at other things.

The successes and failures we have, the people we meet – even our parents, siblings, friends, relatives, bosses, and work colleagues are all a part of our destiny – they were written into our soul print before we were born.

Just recently, I double-parked and sent a friend of mine scurrying into my local deli to buy a particular brand of cheese I adore. She returned to the car breathless and swooning.

'Mitchell, I've just met my future husband,' she said.

Chance encounters, 'goosebump' connections, or 'body tingling' responses towards a person or place are sure signs that the person or place shares a connection with our soul print.

Remember Reannon. Before Jay came into her life, Reannon was convinced her first husband was her soulmate. Naturally, when he asked for a divorce she was devastated. Fortunately, Reannon was able to let go, learn from the experience, and move on with her life.

I encounter stories similar to Reannon's every day. That's why I don't believe there is only ever one perfect soulmate. I prefer to say we have soul connections. I sense there are a number of people we can potentially fall in love with given the right soul print circumstances.

Throughout life, relationships will end and new ones will form. Intuitively, our souls gravitate toward those written into our soul print. Friend or foe, every person is in our life for a reason. They are helping us to learn the lessons we set out in our soul print before we were born. *If*, by chance, we don't learn from our relationships; *if* we don't learn from a difficult demanding parent who pushes us through to success; *if* dealing with a hard critical boss doesn't teach us to stand up for ourselves; *if* we don't learn selfless love from a small child – I sense the same lessons will repeat themselves lifetime and lifetime again.

Our journey back to earth

Have you ever had one of those odd and usually rare moments when the present felt like the past? Have you ever arrived at a place for the first time and felt overwhelmed by the sensation that you've been there before? Perhaps you've met someone for the first time or have been involved in a conversation and heard yourself think, *I've been here before, met this person before and said this before.* I sense in these instances you are recalling fragments from a previous lifetime.

Piper is a prominent lawyer working in Sydney. She is an extremely dedicated, intelligent and spiritually intuitive person.

During an occupational health and safety fire drill, Piper was nominated as the fire warden for her area. Halfway through the practice fire drill, Piper had an anxiety attack. With her heart racing and her breathing in overdrive, she tore off her yellow safety helmet and bolted down the fire escape stairs.

Two weeks later, while sitting in a reading with me, Piper confessed her irrational fear of fire. She couldn't even strike a match or burn a candle. As a result of her anxiety attack during the fire drill, Piper underwent past-life hypnotherapy. To her amazement, she discovered she had burnt to death in a house fire started by a candle.

I believe events and episodes from past lives are stored deep within our soul's memory as individual fragments – much like odd pieces from jigsaw puzzles. Unexpected life events, experiences, feelings, sensations, dreams, thoughts, statements, and emotions can suddenly jar these past-life memory fragments to the surface – connecting your present life with a past-life experience.

Many religions throughout the world believe that the same soul can live many lifetimes. The most celebrated example of reincarnation is the fourteenth Dalai Lama. As a young boy, he correctly identified a range of objects that belonged to him fourteen lifetimes ago.

Vivid recollections of past-life experiences aren't limited to religious figures in foreign countries. Hints and clues pointing toward reincarnation exist in our everyday lives too.

Sonja's four-year-old daughter, Rebecca, was sitting quietly in the corner colouring in. She didn't appear to be paying any attention to the reading in progress. All of a sudden Rebecca interrupted me and said, 'When I was eight me and my baby sister were killed in a car accident.'

'Really,' I said.

'Yes and I went back to Heaven and waited for my new mummy.'

I was speechless.

'I'm not sad because my old mummy comes to visit me at night.'

I turned to Sonja. A look of helplessness washed over her face. 'I've tried to explain to Rebecca that I am her only mummy,' she said.

I sense young children have a stronger recall of their past lives because they have not long been in the physical world.

Another time a friend of mine was running errands. She heard the wail of an ambulance siren. Being a responsible driver, she pulled over so the ambulance could pass safely. Excited by the commotion, her five-year-old daughter unbuckled her seatbelt and stood up on the front seat. As the ambulance raced past, she pointed to it and said, 'I drived one of those, Mummy ... but it was green with a white cross.'

Gobsmacked, my friend asked, 'What do you mean?'

'It was a long, long time ago ... when loud bangs came from the sky,' replied her young daughter.

How incredible, my friend's daughter had no exposure to army life or information relating to World War II, yet she could describe in detail life as an ambulance driver during the war. When my younger brother was the same age, no one could open a car window while travelling. The instant he heard the wind roaring past he'd scream with terror. To this day, I wonder if it is possible that in another life he was sucked out of an aeroplane before it crashed?

I can almost bet that at some stage in your life you've looked into the smiling eyes of a baby and remarked, 'She's an old soul,' or found yourself saying after observing a toddler, 'He's been here before'. These are all clues that many of us have lived life before.

Children are not the only ones who can recall details about past-life experiences. Renowned psychiatrist and author of *Same Soul, Many Bodies* and *Many Lives, Many Masters*, Dr Brian Weiss is a world authority on past lives. He has spent many years analysing vivid past-life recollections given by adults. It comes as no surprise to me that his years of research validate what Spirit has suggested to me all along – some souls have lived many lives.

I am fascinated by the extensive research into birthmarks and the connection they have to previous life times. In Trutz Hardo's book, *Children Who Have Lived Before*, an entire chapter is devoted to children's birthmarks which offers convincing evidence that birthmarks are not always one of nature's oddities.

Several years ago, Mark wrote to me about his four-year-old son Liam. He was born with a white birthmark in the shape of a bald eagle's head near his right shoulder blade. That summer, while Mark was applying extra sunscreen to the birthmark, Liam said, 'Chiefs don't need sunscreen.'

'You're not a chief,' said Mark.

'Not now, silly ... before you were born,' replied Liam.

It was Liam's insistence that he was once a Native American Indian chief that prompted Mark to write to me. Could it be that Liam was an Indian chief in a past life? I wrote back and said it was quite possible.

Instances where the present feels like the past, unusual birthmarks, flashbacks, strange recollections, and sensing strong connections with total strangers are all clues that we have lived life before. Even the lines on the palms of our hands hold clues to our past-life connections. Yet it still leaves one big question. How long does it take before a soul reincarnates?

No one really knows the answer to this question. I sense some souls choose to come back while others choose to stay in the Spirit World. What I can say for sure is that our guardian angels and spirit guides are available to guide, heal, inspire, and protect us. Along with them, our departed loved ones are frequent visitors to our world because they love and miss us. And when they do visit, they usually leave a calling card.

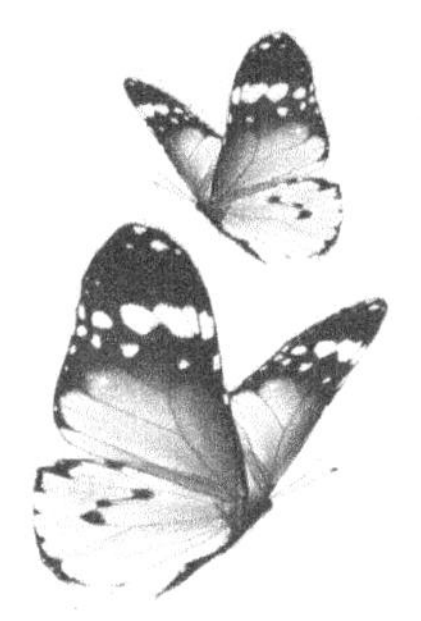

CHAPTER 4

SENSING SPIRIT

Anyone can have mysterious, mystical, and divine encounters with Spirit. Even paranormal events like exploding light bulbs, the appearance of mysterious orbs, changes in temperature and radios that burst into song in the middle of the night can all be messages from Spirit.

Spirit enters the lives of everyone, not just a gifted few. The miracle of love and guidance from Spirit is everywhere – often arriving unannounced, sometimes in dramatic ways, sometimes subtle, yet always memorable.

Spirit can manipulate the air and energy around you in order to materialise, leave you a gift, or even cause a chain reaction of events to save your life – as one Brisbane woman discovered.

In 2003, Lindsay was sitting alone in her broken-down car on the side of the road on a steep decline. The RACQ roadside assistance operator told Lindsay it would take at least forty-five minutes for a mechanic to reach her. Not more than five minutes after placing the call, a man emerged from nowhere. He motioned Lindsay to follow him up the roadside embankment. Lindsay hesitated and looked around for the bright yellow RACQ vehicle. She could not see one. The stranger motioned her more urgently to follow him. A cold shiver ran down her spine. Lindsay locked her doors and watched as the stranger motioned her again. Suddenly, the smell of petrol filled the cabin of her car. No longer feeling safe inside her car, Lindsay unlocked the doors and stepped out.

She knew that if she had a petrol leak one stray cigarette butt flicked out of the window of a passing car could spell disaster. Oddly, Lindsay noted that in the distance she could hear a truck rapidly changing down to lower gears. Why that distant sound, above all others, caught her ear she was not sure. But her immediate concern was ensuring the stranger did not get any closer to her while she determined whether she had a petrol leak or not.

As Lindsay knelt down on the ground and attempted to peer under her car, a small rock hit her in the back of the head. Assuming the stranger had thrown it, Lindsay stood up and yelled, 'What do you think you're doing?'

In that instant, a truck rounded the corner out of control and on a collision course with Lindsay's car. In a split second, Lindsay looked up at the stranger. He beckoned her with more urgency. Impulse took over and Lindsay sprinted straight up the roadside embankment. Behind her came a sickening BANG followed by the sound of crunching metal and smashing glass. She ran even faster up the embankment.

Exhausted but safe, Lindsay turned back in time to see her crumpled car spinning across the road in a shower of sparks. Horrified, Lindsay turned back toward the stranger. He was gone.

Five years later, Lindsay met with me. Unaware of this story, I said, 'A man watches over you from Spirit. He's one of your guides. He's already saved your life once.'

Only once Lindsay had told me the full story did I realise how remarkable her experience was.

Spirit usually only materialises in miraculous ways in times of great need, grief, or danger. Importantly, Spirit will only do so if the materialisation and subsequent intervention does not alter the person's fate or destiny – their soul print.

Materialisation

Two years ago, I was waiting for a flight at an airport lounge. I watched as a gentle woman in her early seventies scanned the sea of passengers. Her soft blue eyes locked onto the empty seat next to me. As she sat down, her vibrant energy filled me with a sense of warmth, much like a loving grandmother. Her eyes twinkled with a youthful enthusiasm as she introduced herself as Dorothy.

'What do you do for a living?' she asked, turning toward me.

I smiled. Experience has taught me answering that question with *I'm a psychic medium* is always met with surprise and uncertainty. But before I could think of what else to say Dorothy said, 'You look like an angel.'

My face lit up with a smile.

'How do you know what an angel looks like?' I asked.

It was Dorothy's turn to smile.

'I was saved by one,' she said with great pride.

Ten years ago, Dorothy was visiting her elderly sister. With her car out of action that day, she decided to catch the bus part of the way and walk the rest. There was one particular section of road she hated crossing. It didn't have pedestrian lights, just a zebra crossing.

Dorothy was halfway across the zebra crossing when she realised a car speeding toward her was not going to stop.

'I just closed my eyes and braced myself for death,' she said.

Dorothy turned slightly, expecting the car to hit her front on, but the impact took her by surprise. An unseen force flew in from the side and knocked her down. *Surely I'm in the hands of death now,* Dorothy recalled thinking to herself. It wasn't until Dorothy felt the wind of the speeding car whistle past her that she realised she was still alive. Shocked and shaken, Dorothy dusted bitumen stones off her grazed knees and inspected her wrists. No bones were broken. Realising someone must have pushed her out of the way, Dorothy turned to thank her saviour. To her surprise she was alone on the zebra crossing. Even the driver of the speeding car hadn't stopped to help.

'That is when I realised I was saved by an angel,' said Dorothy, reaching out to gently grasp my forearm. I smiled and nodded. I have no doubt Spirit saved Dorothy's life that day. It was not her time to pass even though she felt she was in the hands of death.

After one of my shows last year, Gillian told me of an equally miraculous encounter.

Gillian woke to the sensation of someone shaking her awake. The digital clock by her bed read 3.00 a.m. When she opened her eyes her grandfather's fully formed spirit was standing over her. At first, she gasped in fright. On the second gasp, Gillian realised it was not fear making her short of breath. Something was wrong. She could not inhale. Her chest felt tight and constricted. She screamed using all of the remaining air in her lungs, 'Mum – help me.'

Gillian's mum burst into the room and turned on the light.

'What's wrong?'

Gillian struggled to get the words out.

'I – can't – breathe,' she said.

Gillian was prone to severe asthma attacks – often throwing her body into anaphylactic shock. Fortunately, Gillian's grandfather in spirit had woken her in time to raise the alarm.

Spirit is not limited to saving lives. Throughout the world, there are many reports of incidences where Spirit has materialised to offer great comfort in times of extreme grief. I recall an encounter told to me by Leanne.

In 2008, Leanne's four-year-old daughter, Fiona, drowned in the neighbour's swimming pool. It was a horrible twist of fate. Ten adults stood by the poolside that day and more than twenty kids were in and out of the pool, yet not one person noticed or heard Fiona fall in. She drowned in silence – amid the fun and laughter of a poolside barbecue.

Less than two weeks after Fiona's funeral, Leanne woke in the early hours of the morning with that all-too-familiar feeling she was being summoned by a child standing at her bedside. In spite of her mother's instinct, Leanne refused to open her eyes. Sleep was the only time she could escape from the agonising sense of guilt and grief that ripped through her heart every waking moment.

'Fiona is gone, I told myself. But I was still in the habit of being a mum – my mind was instantly operational,' said Leanne. 'So I rolled over onto my side and opened my eyes.'

What Leanne saw next astounded her. Little Fiona was standing beside her.

'Everything about her was real except I could see through her, yet there was no mistaking Fiona's cute pigtails, the dress I buried her in, and her bright smile.'

Leanne attempted to reach out and take

Fiona's small hand, but her entire body was numb. So she just lay in bed marvelling at the sight of her daughter. As she did, she was bathed in a wash of blissful peace and love.

Mummy, I am with Grandma. I love you, Mummy. Miraculously, Fiona's lips did not move yet Leanne heard her voice.

'I cried when Fiona's image faded away, but after a few moments I realised I could still feel her in the room with me,' explained Leanne.

Even though Fiona hasn't materialised since, Leanne can sense each time Fiona pays a visit.

'Fiona's energy vibration makes my skin tingle in a certain way,' explained Leanne. 'It's almost like a personalised ringtone – that all-too-familiar sense of being summoned by a particular child.'

As Leanne discovered, you never know how or when the normal order of things will fall away and a truly miraculous encounter with Spirit will occur. However, I should make it clear that experiences like Leanne's are not everyday occurrences. It takes a tremendous amount of energy for Spirit to materialise into a physical-looking form.

Apparitions

Rarely do departed loved ones choose to materialise into an almost solid full-bodied form as Gillian's grandfather did when he opted to save her from a fatal asthma attack or as little Fiona did when she chose to materialise in order to ease her mother's overwhelming guilt and grief. Instead, Spirit may appear as a fleeting glimpse out of the corner of your eye, as a flash of someone reflected in a shiny surface, or as a departed loved one among a crowd.

While driving past a sign that read 'Antique Road Show Today', Chloe, a friend of mine, was thinking of her dearly departed father. He absolutely loved antique road shows. Chloe thought to herself, *Dad would so be at this show if he were alive*. In that instant, Chloe spotted a figure moving within the sea of people flowing toward the entrance to the show. Her dad's signature red felt hat and herringbone jacket with leather patches on the sleeves were unmistakable.

Chloe told herself she must be crazy, but tooted the car horn anyway and yelled, 'Dad,' while waving madly. The figure turned, gave a cheeky grin, and vanished into thin air. Chloe stared in disbelief. Two strangers waved back at her.

Spirit has the playful inventiveness of a child and will always find a way to catch your attention and deliver a message.

John's father died from a heart attack when John was just fifteen years old. That left John, his younger brother, and his mother to run the cattle farm.

'They were tough times,' explained John. 'Mum became overly anxious about me. She thought I was not grieving properly.'

John's mum's anxiety probably had a lot to do with John repeatedly saying, 'Dad is still with us.'

'The first time it happened I was sitting in the farm ute,' explained John. 'When I turned the ignition key, nothing happened. There wasn't even the click-click of a flat battery.'

Angry, John turned the ignition key repeatedly – despite realising the engine was unlikely to start. Finally giving up, John thumped the steering wheel, screwed his eyes and screamed out a swear word.

Feeling his temper pass, John opened his eyes again. In that moment, his father's face flashed onto the rear-view mirror.

'He was laughing at me,' explained John. 'So I turned the ignition key again and the ute engine started – just like that.'

John's father was always tampering with the ute engine. It was his way of having fun and teaching John how to troubleshoot an engine with starting problems.

'No other sign would have given me as much faith Dad was still with me,' said John.

Knowing that his dad was riding in the ute with him, even though he was in spirit, filled John with a great sense of peace and love.

Interestingly, many cultures in the world consider mirrors a gateway into magic, the supernatural, the soul and mysteries of the universe.

Reese Witherspoon spoke of a time when she saw her dearly departed grandfather. She was doing a play reading in New York. There was hardly anybody watching. When she looked out during the play, her grandfather was sitting watching her. She looked down for a second and when she looked up again, he was gone.

In most cases, an apparition appears as a fleeting figure. Even so, most people catch enough visual information to identify who among their loved ones passed is trying to make contact. Often sightings coincide with tingling sensations and a comforting warm feeling throughout the body. However, what is even more common is to experience *spirit touch.*

Many people have felt a soft reassuring hand on their shoulder, a gentle kiss on their cheek, or a comforting hug from Spirit. How and when these beautiful things happen depends on what you've asked for during your quiet whisperings to Spirit. 'I wish Mum was here to see this.' 'If only Dad could show me he is okay.' 'I hope there are toys in Heaven for my child to play with.'

Spirit touch

When you experience *spirit touch*, you'll feel a concentration of warmth or coolness in one place on your body. If a departed loved one is standing close, you may feel cold on one side of your body – goosebumps may even appear.

Two years after losing her mother, Julia's life was still on hold. One day she was standing at her gas cooktop stirring a pot of soup. All of a sudden, she felt two warm hands place themselves between her shoulder blades and gently push her forward.

The following morning, Julia was still unable to make sense of the feeling, so she rang me. I suggested it was time for a reading.

Later that afternoon, she arrived. As we walked into my reading room, I asked if she had brought something that belonged to the person in spirit she most hoped to make contact with. Julia handed me a small framed photograph of her mother. My connection was immediate.

'I feel like your mum is gently pushing you along. It's her way of saying, *Julia, it's time to move on with your life.*'

Even I am subject to prods and pokes from Spirit. Some time ago, I was on stage giving readings. As usual, there was a queue of dearly departed eager to get through to their loved ones in the audience. One persistent and rather impatient spirit kept stomping her umbrella. Tap, tap, tap was all I could hear while I was conveying messages for others. It was more annoying than listening to a dripping tap in the middle of the night. Finally, I had to turn around and say, 'You just wait your turn.' Well, the audience thought that was hilarious. There I was turning around chastising a persistent spirit like a parent disciplining a child constantly interrupting a conversation.

Not at all impressed with my response, the woman in spirit poked me repeatedly in the back with her umbrella. I was saying, 'Ouch, ouch and ouch,' while performing a crazy back-arching moonwalk across the stage. The audience applauded my impromptu performance.

As if that was not bad enough, in my teen years Spirit used to give me taps and slaps. One tap on the back of my neck meant information was ready to come through from Spirit. And if by chance I did not interpret the images, sounds and signs correctly, Spirit would gently slap me on the forehead. Talk about firm coaching! It used to drive me mad.

Now, of course, things are very different. I have developed an entire system of symbols that allow me to filter what is coming through from Spirit without the need for Spirit to tap and slap to indicate the correct interpretation.

Just as Spirit can give a 'gentle push' for all the right reasons, Spirit can also hug – as my mum and I discovered.

Not only is my mum a guiding light in my life, she has been for others too. She is a wonderful caring person. When our next-door neighbour was dying, Mum was there to help in any way she could.

One night Mum was standing at the kitchen sink washing the dishes. I was next to her drying them. We were chatting about the day when Mum suddenly gasped, dropped the dish she was washing into the soapy water and grasped hold of the bench. 'Mitchell, note the time,' she managed to say. 'It might be symbolic.' Panicked, I glanced at the microwave clock. It read 7.07 p.m. I was about to reach out and help Mum when I too gasped for breath. I suddenly felt someone grab me tightly around the waist and whiz me into the air like a small child. In my mind I could see a much younger version of our next-door neighbour. She loved to give me 'whizzies' when I was a kid. Then as suddenly as it happened, the sensation passed for both Mum and I.

The next day, my next-door neighbour's daughter phoned.

'I am so sorry to tell you this … Mum passed away peacefully in her sleep last night.'

'What time?' I heard Mum ask.

Seven minutes past seven was her answer.

During the 2009 Mind Body Spirit Festival in Sydney, Maxine related a fabulous 'hug' encounter to me.

In the dead of night, Maxine woke suddenly. She sat up in bed, collected her wits, and decided to check on her six-year-old daughter, Bella.

As Maxine pushed gently on Bella's partially open bedroom door, she was surprised to see her daughter sitting up in bed.

'At first I couldn't work out what Bella was doing,' explained Maxine. 'Her arms were extended as if she were miming giving someone a hug.'

Maxine was about to walk in and settle Bella down when she heard the phone ring.

She ran back to her bedroom. When she entered the bedroom, the bedside light was on. Her husband motioned the phone call was for her. Maxine took the phone from her husband's outstretched hand and sat down on the edge of the bed. Her husband shuffled across the bed and sat next to her, placing his arm around her shoulders. Only then did Maxine realise it was the phone call they had both been dreading.

'Mrs Robinson, this is nurse Rosemary Williams. Your mother passed away five minutes ago. Would you like to come to the hospital?'

Maxine dressed and left her husband to organise the car while she went to wake Bella.

'What is it, Mummy?' asked Bella, before Maxine got a chance to turn on the light.

'Bella, why are you still awake?' asked Maxine.

'Grandma woke me. She gave me a big hug. Is she going on a holiday?'

Maxine scooped Bella up into her arms and burst into tears.

Young children can sense Spirit and see further than most adults can. Their young minds are still pure – untainted by religious dogma, or conditioned by social and cultural beliefs. A child's world is one of vivid imaginations, open-mindedness, and a shared connectedness to the Spirit World.

Jenny, a friend of mine, shared a wonderful memory of her grandma being 'kissed by a ghost' – as she put it.

When Jenny was ten years old, she usually found herself sitting quietly with her grandmother at the same time every evening. Seated in front of the dresser mirror, her grandmother would unwind a long plait of grey hair she had secured in a tight bun. She would pick up her hairbrush and say, 'Your poppy gave this to me as an engagement present.' Jenny would ask, 'Why do you always brush your hair over to one side?' and Jenny's grandma would answer, 'So your poppy can kiss me goodnight on the cheek.'

After brushing her hair, Jenny's grandma would put the hairbrush down, close her eyes and tilt her left cheek upward. Sometimes she'd sit there like that for ten minutes. Jenny knew not to disturb her until she opened her eyes again. When she did, Jenny would ask, 'Did Poppy kiss you?' Her grandma would always smile and nod.

'But I didn't see him,' Jenny would say.

'That's because he's a ghost,' Jenny's grandma would reply.

It was like a well-rehearsed play with the same questions and answers – one that lasted up until Jenny moved out of home at the age of twenty.

Many years later, when Jenny's grandma lay dying in her hospital bed, Jenny sat brushing her grandma's hair as best she could.

'Did Poppy kiss you on the cheek last night?' Jenny asked.

Jenny's grandma smiled and nodded feebly.

'But I didn't see him,' whispered Jenny into her grandma's ear.

'That's because he's a ghost,' Jenny's grandma answered in a weak voice.

'And tonight, will Poppy kiss you tonight?'

Jenny's grandma shook her head sideways. Jenny stopped brushing.

'How come?' she asked, surprised.

'Tonight, he kisses my hand and then I go with him.'

Jenny's grandma passed peacefully in the early hours of the next morning.

Many more people experience the glorious touch of Spirit upon falling asleep or just before waking. Spirit often chooses that time because the mind and body is at rest and most receptive to a hello from the other side.

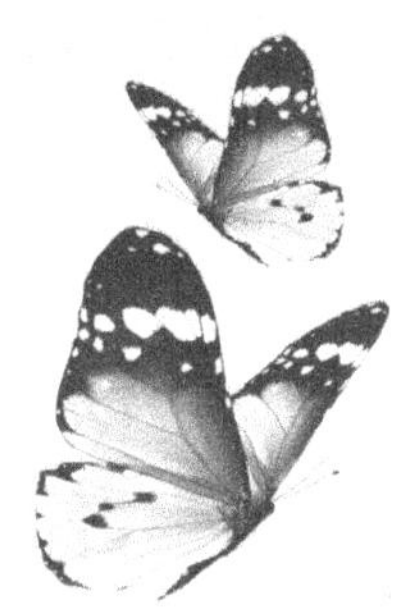

CHAPTER 5

SENSING THE EXTRAORDINARY

There are times when Spirit will resort to dramatic paranormal measures to grab your attention. This is often a time when your own belief system may challenge you.

Rapping, tapping, and knocking noises

Not so long ago Mark, a 51-year-old man, sat in front of me with his wife, Verna. Four years ago, a series of strange paranormal knockings appeared to be haunting Mark and Verna.

'It was three sets of three distinct knocks,' attested Mark.

'The knocks seemed to originate above Mark's head,' added Verna.

'They were firm, loud and sounded like someone using their knuckles to knock on the wood headboard above me,' explained Mark.

Oddly, the knocking occurred three nights in a row and then stopped.

'Nothing notable happened after that until last week,' explained Mark. 'The knocking started again.'

I knew why. I had linked up with the spirit responsible within moments of Mark and Verna sitting down.

'Who haven't you thought of in a while?' I asked.

Both Mark and Verna looked at me blankly.

'I'll give you a clue. When did the knocking start?'

'After Mark's father passed,' answered Verna.

'Yes, and what was significant about last week?'

Mark and Verna looked at each other, unsure. Finally, the penny dropped for Verna.

'Oh … it was the anniversary of your dad's passing, Mark. We completely forgot,' said Verna, turning to Mark. 'We've been so busy.'

Spirit is renowned for creating paranormal activity – especially if they have exhausted all other means of gaining your attention. Ghostly goings-on are mostly nothing more than a reminder from Spirit. It's Spirit's way of saying, *I'm just as much a part of your life today as I was when I was in the living world.*

Later into the reading, I was able to confirm for Mark and Verna that the phantom knocking was indeed Mark's father. He was simply trying to make them aware he was concerned for them. He was worried about how busy and stressed their lives had become. *Remember the little things that make life a pleasure*, he communicated.

Departed loved ones are not the only souls who can rap, and knock to get your attention. Dearly departed pets can be as inventive, if not mischievous.

Vicky sat in front of me, a frightened, nervous wreck. Her skin looked pale, accentuating the dark rings under her eyes. She wrung her hands while recounting her experience. You didn't need to be psychic to tell she hadn't been sleeping well.

'For the past four weeks an eerie tap, tap, tap sound has woken me,' explained Vicky. 'The first time it happened I just hid under my doona. I thought an intruder had broken into my room.'

By the second week, Vicky's fear had given way to frustration.

'I discovered that as soon as I turned on my bedside light, the tapping stopped,' explained Vicky. 'So I tried sleeping with the light on.'

That worked for about two nights.

'On the third night I woke screaming. Something had landed on the end of my bed,' she said.

Vicky's flatmate heard her scream. She burst into the room just as Vicky scrambled out of bed.

'What is it? A spider?'

'No,' said Vicky, pointing at the dimple that had formed in her doona.

Vicky's flatmate turned tail and ran out of the room.

'I was shocked. The dimple felt warm. It was like a hot water bottle had been resting there for a few minutes,' she explained. 'But I was even more surprised when my flatmate returned with her camera.'

'What are you doing?' asked Vicky.

'Checking whether it's a message from Spirit,' answered her paranormal-hunting flatmate.

At that point, Vicky reached into her handbag and slid two photographs taken by her flatmate across the table toward me. In the first photograph, a small semi-transparent sphere was visible above her dressing table. In the second photograph, another sphere hung suspended centimetres above the dimple in the doona.

'I'm hearing the name Matilda, does that mean anything to you?' I asked.

'I don't think so. No aunts or relatives with that name,' she responded.

'Are you sure?' I asked.

'The only Matilda I know of is my cat, but she passed six weeks ago.'

In my mind's eye, I could see Matilda's fluffy white paw whacking a hard plastic ball tethered on a string. It made the sound of tap,

tap, tap as the ball knocked against the wall.

Dearly loved pets, just like loved ones, will find ways to let you know they have made it to the Afterlife and have linked up with other family members or pets.

It gave me great pleasure to reassure Vicky the tapping and phantom sensation of something landing on her bed was just Matilda. It wasn't a ghost. Matilda had simply come back to say hello because she knew Vicky was missing her.

Incredibly, Matilda had left Vicky with a gift of two photographs. Featured in each was Matilda's spirit in the form of a semi-transparent orb. How amazing is that?

In the last ten years, there has been a dramatic increase in the number of people seeing or photographing spirit lights and orbs.

Spirit lights

Spirit lights are a reaction to the energy produced by Spirit in the early stages of manifestation in the physical world. Spirit lights can appear as semi-transparent spheres, sparks of light, gauze-like strips, or a luminous mist. The colour is rarely static and may alternate from white through to hints of blue, yellow, orange and even violet. Some spirit lights appear accompanied by the sound of a high vibration hum.

It takes an enormous amount of energy for a spirit to materialise in the physical world. However, forming as a spirit light or orb takes far less energy and lasts longer. That is why sightings of spirit lights are more common.

Many people report seeing spirit lights minutes before falling asleep or during deep meditation. Sightings occur mostly in the peripheral vision. Children, however, often experience more profound encounters.

Six months ago, Nancy arrived for her reading.

'Mitchell, I hope you don't mind, but I've brought Sigrid with me. I was hoping you could make sense of what happened to her.'

Two weeks before the reading, Nancy had taken Sigrid riverbank fishing. Although fishing was a sacred father–daughter activity, Nancy often broke tradition.

'Sigrid's dad is a fly-in and fly-out worker,' Nancy explained. 'When he's away she misses him terribly. Fishing seems to help her.'

As a rule, Nancy kept their fishing adventures to day trips, but this time she decided to camp overnight. Sigrid announced she was going down to the river's edge to fill up her bucket. Nancy watched as Sigrid danced off. The kettle boiling on the gas stove began to whistle. Nancy ignored it. Instead, she watched Sigrid scoop up water in her bucket, turn around, and start walking back toward her. Only then did Nancy attend to the kettle and make herself a cup of tea.

Nancy had taken her eyes off Sigrid for less than four minutes, yet when she looked up, Sigrid was nowhere in sight. Only her bright blue bucket stood halfway between the riverbank and their tent. And to make matters worse, twilight was rapidly giving way to the darkness of night.

'I did my best to hold back my panic, Sigrid was a devil for playing hide-and-seek unannounced,' Nancy explained.

'Sigrid, where are you? Come out, come out, wherever you are.'

Silence answered. Nancy called again.

'Sigrid, this is not funny. Come out – now!' yelled Nancy.

Again, there was no answer – only the unnerving murmurs of waterbirds as they settled in some invisible place for the night.

Grabbing a torch, Nancy ran. *Oh God no – not the river,* she thought. Her heart sank as she made herself scan the still water.

'Sigrid, call out to Mummy. You're frightening me.'

Luckily, four other campers were nearby. Hearing Nancy's desperate calls, they offered to help search for Sigrid. By this time, it was dark.

Nancy was beside herself. Calling the SES was not an option. There was no mobile phone reception. Someone would have to get into their car and drive to get help.

At that moment, Sigrid came bounding through the low scrub back toward the river and campsite.

'"There she is," I heard a voice yell. But the amazing thing was, Mitchell, that not once did her step falter. It was pitch black. We were all using torches and Sigrid came running toward me as if it were broad daylight,' explained Nancy.

'I'm here, Mummy.'

'Be careful! You'll fall and hurt yourself,' Nancy warned, shining her torch to light her daughter's path.

'No I won't, Mummy. The angel gave me an orange ball of light to follow.'

Children are innately psychic because they

are still so fresh from the spirit realm. So it did not surprise me Sigrid was guided back to safety by Spirit.

Spirit photography

The language of Spirit has no boundaries. Even a curious white 'sphere', an 'unusual smear', or an 'intriguing spiral of mist' that mysteriously appears in a birthday, wedding, or holiday photograph can be a message from Spirit. Today, more than any other time throughout history, photographs capturing spirit lights – especially as spherical orbs – are being taken by ordinary people all over the world. As a result, there is much debate about whether orbs are just dust or moisture particles on the lens, or whether they are true signs that Spirit is present and trying to communicate. I believe that in certain circumstances the capturing of orbs in photographs and camcorders is genuine.

Unlike spirit lights, spirit orbs are rarely

visible to the naked eye. They are mostly caught on digital and infra-red cameras, CCTV and webcams. This is due to the advancement of digital technology.

Today, camera processors are so sensitive to light energy they can capture what was invisible to the naked eye at the time of taking the photograph. That's why so many people only discover an orb-like sphere or gauze-like mist *after* the picture has been taken.

Of course capturing orb-like phenomena in photographs is not limited to family events, birthdays or special occasions. By taking random photographs near ruins, sacred sites, or natural wonders you may also capture evidence of spirit activity unrelated to you. If you do, remember that it is no coincidence that you pushed the shutter button when you did.

If you are keen to photograph spirit lights or orbs there is no real need to rush out and buy an expensive camera. I've seen some fantastic orb shots taken on a disposable camera.

If Spirit intends you to see them in a photograph – you will.

The key component in spirit photography is your intuition, not the camera. Successful spirit photography is about listening to the inner voice – the one that urges you to take the photo *now*.

Incredibly, phantom-like figures, spirit anomalies and semi-transparent replicas of loved ones passed can manifest in photographs days, weeks, or even years later. The tech savvy among you may have already discovered this after downloading your photographs into photo-viewing software. After enlarging photographs of orbs many people have reported identifying a face within the orb that has a startling resemblance to a loved one passed. Either way it is always a good idea to revisit your favourite photographs. If you ask me, it's the perfect thing to do on a cold winter's day while sipping a cup of hot chocolate.

Manipulating photographs is not the only

form of physical-world contact Spirit can make. Amazingly, Spirit can use its energy to interrupt the working of electrical devices to draw your attention to their presence.

Paranormal electrical disturbances

Light bulbs, radios, televisions, CD players and other household appliances are not beyond Spirit manipulation – as my long-time friend Susan discovered.

Susan's mum was an accomplished pianist, but her passion was for gathering everyone around the piano to sing old traditional hymns. 'In the Garden' was her favourite – especially the gospel version sung by Elvis Presley. Yet, as much as she loved the hymn, she lamented that it was too slow. She felt an upbeat version would be more fitting to such a beautiful hymn.

Sadly, Susan's mum passed. Naturally, Susan chose to play Elvis Presley's version of

'In the Garden' at the funeral service.

The minister reached into his cassock, removed the remote control, and pointed it at the church sound system. The first few opening bars of music played, then all of a sudden the CD player faltered. Elvis's voice burst through the speakers singing at chipmunk speed, 'I come to the garden alone while the dew is still on the roses ...'

Susan laughed aloud. As sad as the occasion was, it was her moment of validation. Her mum was with her still, albeit in spirit. And as soon as Susan made that acknowledgment, the music played at the correct tempo – much to the minister's relief.

On another occasion, Susan and I were chatting over dinner. I was recalling the many incredible paranormal events reported to me over the years. Knowing how much I love a mystery, Susan said to me with a twinkle in her eye, 'I have something very mysterious happening at home, but you need to see it for yourself.'

When we arrived at Susan's home after dinner, she led me straight into a bedroom. She drew back the ceiling-to-floor drapes covering a window.

'This will all make sense in a moment,' she said. 'Mum is here. Come and look.'

I walked over to where Susan was standing and peered out through the window into the night.

'No, not out there, Mitchell. Down there,' laughed Susan, pointing at the floor.

Plugged into a power point near the floor was a night light. It emitted a soft, muted orange glow.

'Ask Mum a question,' Susan suggested. 'The light is how Mum has been communicating with me.'

Just then, the light flickered softly as if attempting to answer my question. Intrigued, I bent down to inspect the night light. The power switch was off, yet each time I put my hand near it, the light grew stronger and whiter.

'What happens if I turn the power on?' I asked.

'Nothing,' answered Susan. 'It just gives a constant glow like it's supposed to.'

Susan later told me her uncle is an electrician and he tested for a power leak. He found nothing. Her brother is an electrical engineer and even he was baffled as to why the night light was flickering and able to change intensity without a direct power source.

On some nights, the night light would glow and wake Susan. In a dreamy state she'd open one eye, look at the light, smile and fall back to sleep knowing her mum was watching over her.

'I sense your mum spent a lot of time in this room before she passed,' I said to Susan.

'Yes, this is the only room she could see all of her beautiful garden from.'

There were many nights when the light did not glow for Susan. On those occasions, Susan had prayed to her mum. Susan asked that her mum spend time with her sister because she was going through a rough patch in her life. Susan's sister needed love, comfort, and guidance from her mum in spirit more than Susan did at that time.

Spirit is not always with you when you ask. Just like you and I in our daily lives, Spirit also has many special Spirit World duties to perform. Whether that be saving a person from a certain death as in Lindsay's case when her car broke down, or preventing a premature death as in Dorothy's case on the zebra crossing, Spirit will be where it is most important according to the person's unique soul print.

Not so long ago a fifty-year-old woman named Abbie came to me for a reading. She also had a wonderful experience concerning Spirit and electricity.

Three months after burying her beloved husband, Bob, Abbie was convinced she was losing her mind. 'When Bob passed, a part of me died with him,' she said. 'I miss him terribly. He was my soulmate.'

To ease her grief, Abbie created what she called 'Bob's Prayer Path'. Each evening when she returned home from work, she would walk the same path through the house, just as Bob did when he was alive.

'My two sons thought I had gone mad with grief,' she confessed.

During 'Bob's Prayer Path' Abbie would unlock the front door, enter the hallway, and turn on the light. Being an older Tudor-style home, the hallways were dark no matter what time of day it was. With the hallway light on, Abbie would remove her shoes, walk to the laundry, and turn on the light before washing her hands. With her hands clean and dry she would then walk into the kitchen, fill the kettle with water, switch it on and shout, 'I'm home'. While waiting for the kettle to boil, Abbie would chat to Bob and tell him about her day – as if he were in the kitchen with her; just as he had done when he was alive.

'My prayer path always ended with the

same thought, *I wish there was some way I could know if you can hear me, Bob,*' Abbie explained.

Then one day, three months after Bob's passing, Abbie came home and every single light bulb on 'Bob's Prayer Path' exploded with a POP! The first time it happened she ignored it and just replaced the light globes. But by the fourth time within as many weeks she decided to call in an electrician to check out the wiring.

Abbie called Bob's friend Pete. The two of them had worked together for years.

'Abbie, the wiring is fine,' said Pete, as he wriggled out of the manhole and placed his feet on the ladder.

Once on the ground Pete took Abbie's hand, patting it reassuringly. 'It's probably old Bob just letting you know he's still keeping an eye on you.'

'Mitchell, I just stared at Pete dumbfounded. *Of course it's Bob,* I thought.'

Of all the electrical devices in the world,

radios are the most tampered with by Spirit. I've had clients whose radios, and televisions for that matter, suddenly turn on or off by themselves.

One client reported suffering from post-natal depression after the birth of her second baby. During her darkest days, the family-room radio used to turn on by itself. Amazingly, each time it came on she'd hear the words, 'Blue skies, nothing but blue skies smiling down on me ...' Not only were they the opening lyrics to Willie Nelson's hit song 'Blue Skies', but her grandfather used to sing those exact words to her as a child. He called it his happy song.

Spirit has also been known to interfere with telephones and mobile phones. I have experienced this myself. On one occasion, my telephone rang at an hour when I knew it could only be bad news. I sprang out of bed to answer it. When I got to it, no one was on the other end. I listened and all I heard was static. I noted the time but nothing significant eventuated the next day – unlike Cheryl's experience.

Cheryl's husband was a linesman working for a power company. He and his crew were working one block away. Cheryl was busy making his lunch, expecting him home any moment. A loud BANG reverberated through her house, shaking her windows. In that instant, all the power went out, yet her digital phone started to ring. She looked at the caller ID panel. It read 'HUBBY'. She picked up the receiver, 'Hi darling'. Among the loud burst of static, she heard the faint words, 'Love you'. Suddenly, the phone line was dead.

Six minutes later an ambulance siren that had been wailing in the distance raced past her house. Eight minutes later, there was a knock at her front door. As she opened the door her heart sank and her knees weakened. One of her husband's work crew stood in front of her.

'Cheryl, there's been a terrible accident. You need to come with me.'

The loud bang Cheryl had heard earlier was a power pole transformer exploding. Her husband was working on it at the time. He died instantly.

In the split second of his passing Cheryl's husband combined spirit energy with the excess of electricity to make one last 'I love you' call to Cheryl. There is no end to the ingenious nature of Spirit, especially when it comes to impressing sounds and voices on recording devices.

The American Association of Electronic Voice Phenomena documents many cases on its website where spirit voices have impressed themselves on magnetic tapes, answering machines, and computer recording software. Often the person who discovers an unexpected electronic voice projection (EVP) usually has no idea how or when the voice recording occurred.

Interestingly, in nearly all unexpected EVP recordings, the individual involved asked their departed loved one to make contact in some way. Generally, EVPs left by departed loved ones are short phrases only – no more than four words. The voice is usually very faint and barely audible above static.

To speak, materialise, or rap and tap on walls, a spirit needs to gather a lot of energy. Spirit energy is measurable by using an electromagnetic field (EMF) meter. The meter will register when Spirit is nearby, indicating abnormal fluctuations in the electromagnetic vibration within a given area.

I recall the time I visited Sydney's Manly Quarantine Station – reputedly one of the most haunted sites in Australia. My friend and I rushed ahead of the tour group eager to try out my new EMF meter. Sensing Spirit, I stopped and held my EMF meter in front of me. Initially, the line of coloured LED lights didn't register a thing. Suddenly, the EMF lights lit up – one, two, three, four. And as suddenly as they lit up they went out – four, three, two, one. This pattern repeated several times, giving me the impression a spirit was marching up and down in front of me.

When the tour guide caught up to where I was standing, he turned to the rest of the group and said, 'There have been reports of a ghost marching up and down here.' I smiled, happy that my EMF meter had worked.

Apporting – gifts from the Afterlife

Spirit has an extraordinary ability to make solid objects like flowers, feathers, jewellery, little crystals, or small coins seemingly appear out of thin air. Known as apports, objects transported by Spirit are heavenly gifts.

Due to the enormous energy required by Spirit to dematerialise an object, transport it through the Spirit World and rematerialise it in another place and time, apports are to be treasured. Encapsulated in each apport is a special message.

Six months after a long and bitter divorce, another client of mine recalled finding a single white gardenia on her doorstep. The delicate flower flooded her mind with memories of a wonderful man she had met while working away. The chemistry between them was immediate. So much so, within two days of meeting her, he gave her the most beautiful bouquet of white gardenias she had ever seen. But she was engaged to be married. Consequently, she respectfully kept her distance and returned home to marry her fiancé.

The single white gardenia my client found on her doorstep was a message. 'Spirit is telling me that love is about to walk back through your door,' I said.

Seven months later, my client rang with much excitement in her voice. She'd just returned from an overseas conference – one she would have not attended if her fellow colleague had not fallen ill. Attending the same conference was the same wonderful man from all those years ago who'd given her the bunch of white gardenias.

Equally, Spirit can make objects disappear into thin air. The disappearance of a much-loved ring, locket, or bracelet can be heartbreaking, but there is always a good reason – as Bernadette discovered.

Bernadette treasured her mother's wedding ring. It didn't gleam with an eighteen-carat gold shine as you might expect. Instead, the antique rose gold was dull and slightly tarnished. In some sections, the band had worn and it threatened to break each time Bernadette tried it on. That didn't bother Bernadette because the ring symbolised three generations of hard-working women – her grandmother, her mother, and now herself.

Each morning Bernadette would remove the ring from her jewellery box, kiss it, and send her love to her mother and grandmother in spirit. Then one morning the ring was gone. Bernadette frantically searched her home. She interrogated her husband and pleaded with her children to help search for it. Even their adorable Labrador joined in the search. He sniffed and barked throughout the house. No one could find it. The ring had mysteriously vanished. Distraught, Bernadette dropped her children off at the bus stop and continued to work.

Sadly, the ring didn't turn up the next morning as Bernadette had hoped. However, upon returning home that afternoon, Bernadette opened her front door to discover someone had broken in. All her jewellery, the children's laptops, CDs, DVDs, and iPods were missing. Naturally, she phoned the police.

When the insurance assessor arrived the next morning to assess the robbery, Bernadette showed him to the empty jewellery box sitting on her dressing table. She even upended the box to make her point.

'See, they took everything,' she said.

'Not quite everything,' said the assessor, bending over to pick something up off the floor.

To Bernadette's astonishment, the assessor placed her mother's worn, antique rose gold ring in the palm of her hand.

'Not worth much,' he said. 'I guess that's why they didn't bother to pick it up.'

Bernadette was overjoyed. The return of her mother's ring meant more to her than all her jewellery put together.

I believe Bernadette's mother knew the robbery was going to happen. That's why she temporarily apported the ring for safekeeping. But, more importantly, it was a sign that Bernadette's mum was watching over her. A friend of mine, Suzy, had a similar experience.

For as long as Suzy could remember, her father always wore a checked Havana trilby hat. Wearing it became his signature trait. When he passed, Suzy would often hold onto his hat and feel that his spirit was close by.

Suzy kept the hat safe on a shelf in the laundry. Every morning while ironing her clothes for work she'd talk to her dad. But one morning, the hat was gone. Suzy tore the house apart frantically searching and asking, 'Dad, where is your hat?'

Having not found the hat, distressed and late for work, Suzy jumped into her car and drove off. While driving Suzy happened to glance at pedestrians walking along the footpath when something caught her eye. Among the pedestrians, she noticed a checked hat just like her dad's.

'Dad?' she said. 'It can't be.'

Not only was the hat the same but so was the man's profile. He walked strong and proud like her dad. Suzy was so sure it was him, her heart started racing and tears welled up in her eyes. But when she took a second look, he was gone.

Later that evening Suzy returned home and searched the house again. With her dad's hat nowhere to be found, she went into the laundry. While putting a load of laundry into the washing machine she looked up. There on the shelf was her dad's hat safe.

What a powerful validation for Suzy. The mysterious disappearance and reappearance of her dad's hat was his way of getting her attention to remind her that he was close by and watching over her.

Two years ago, despite her own financial hardships, another client of mine was volunteering at a Red Cross op shop. While sorting through a huge pile of donated clothes, an old three-quarter length army coat grabbed her attention. As she picked it up, a round object fell from one of the pockets. Picking it up, my client discovered the object was an Australian penny, dated 1945. Shiny and worn thin on one side, it looked like whoever owned the penny used to rub it like a lucky charm.

Convinced the penny was indeed a lucky charm sent from Heaven, she asked a jeweller to turn the penny into a pendant. She told all those who asked about her odd-looking pendant that it was her personal sign of prosperity. Three weeks later, she won over six thousand dollars. The money could not have come at a better time.

I have no shame in picking up a coin off the street, even if it is just a five-cent piece. That is because I often ask Spirit for validation in sets of three. When I was much younger, I wasn't sure whether to invest my last five hundred dollars in a new set of tyres for my car. The tread on my old ones was dangerously low and winter was fast approaching. So I asked Spirit to show me a sign. I specifically asked for three coins. If they appeared within quick succession it was a sign that my financial circumstances would improve. I wouldn't starve if I spent my money on new tyres. That afternoon I found five cents lying on the ground near the driver's door of my car.

The next day, I took the last sip of my hot chocolate, stood up to leave the café and found fifty cents on the table. That night I was dressed to go out. I slipped my foot into my shoe only to discover a flat disc-like lump inside. When I investigated, I found a two-dollar coin. Today, finding three coins is a sure sign from Spirit that my course of action is the correct one.

I recall one woman who came to me for a reading. She complained she was always struggling to make the financial ends of her business meet. I asked her if she ever found coins lying on the ground. 'All the time,' she said, 'but I never pick them up.' I said to her, 'If you don't collect what Spirit gives you along the way, how can you possibly expect to receive any more?'

The message associated with apported objects may not always be clear at first. Finding a coin may not always mean more 'money' is coming your way. Sometimes it is the date that is important because it coincides with a birthday or anniversary. Other times it may be a departed loved one's way of saying my thoughts are with you on your special day.

The Spirit World works in the most unusual ways and there are no guarantees as to *where* and *when* Spirit will show. Keep in mind that, instead of direct answers, Spirit may send messages that are more like riddles. When that happens, Spirit is saying you have to do some of the work interpreting the pieces of the psychic puzzle – much like a game of spiritual charades. But know that when the divine timing is right, Spirit will call.

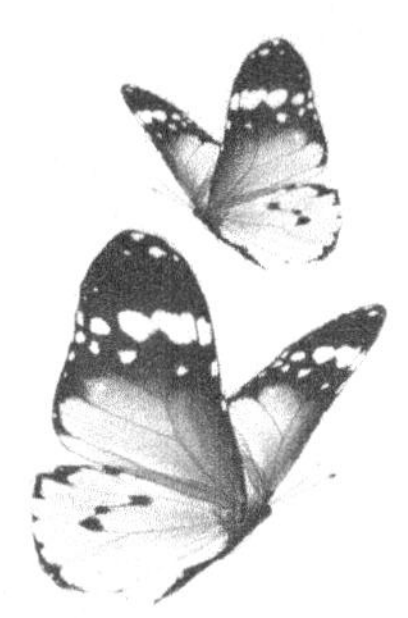

CHAPTER 6

AFTERLIFE RINGTONES

Have you ever been at work or in a meeting and turned your mobile phone to silent, only to realise hours later that you've missed a number of calls because you couldn't hear the phone ringing? Or perhaps you changed the ringtone and then didn't answer because the sound was unfamiliar to you. Guess what? Every day many of us miss calls from Spirit for the very same reason. We simply do not recognise the Afterlife ringtone.

We fail to pick up and answer. Thankfully, Spirit and our loved ones passed never give up calling.

Loved ones in the Afterlife go to enormous lengths to call and message us. They take a keen interest in our lives. They will assist us whenever they can – especially in moments of great need, or when we require comfort and reassurance.

The trouble is, when the Afterlife phone rings most of us don't recognise the ringtone. We don't *see, hear,* or *feel* a thing. And if we do, we say things like, 'Wow, wasn't that a lucky break,' or, 'Gee – what a coincidence.' There is no such thing as a coincidence. Nothing happens by chance. And even though it may not be obvious at the time, there is a reason for everything.

Too many people attribute spirit-inspired events to coincidence. This is mostly because of the *way* Spirit places calls to us. Just for a moment, imagine you have crossed over into the Afterlife. As a result, you no longer have a physical body – only a spirit body. That presents you with many new challenges, but one in particular. Just *how* do you communicate with your living loved ones from your new environment?

On your first attempt to call your loved one, you decide to muster all your energy to create the sensation of *touch.* To your amazement, your loved one *feels* your touch but then passes the sensation off as nothing.

Next, you decide to go and visit. The trouble is the dog is the only one to sense your presence. He barks wildly with excitement. His mission is to let *everyone* in the family know that *you* are there. But when your family investigates, they find the dog barking at thin air. The only thing they're left questioning is the dog's odd behaviour.

On the next attempt to call, you decide to make the lights flicker. All that achieves for your loved one is a stack of exorbitant call-out fees from the electrician.

Next, you decide to *pop* into your loved

one's dream because you have an important message. She or he wakes the next morning and passes it all off as *only a dream.*

As you can see there are so many ways for Spirit to call us but we need to keep an open mind as to how the message will come through.

A year or so ago, after presenting at the Mind Body Spirit Festival in Sydney, a woman with the most striking blue eyes rushed up to me. She was desperate to know why her father had not given her a sign from the Afterlife.

'I meditate daily, talk to his photo and look after his vintage car,' she explained. 'I think about him every day – yet nothing. I'm worried he's had trouble crossing over.'

In my experience, setting up expectations or trying too hard to receive a spirit-inspired message will limit your chance of sensing calls from the Afterlife. There is no time, as we understand it, in the Afterlife. An answer from Spirit could be received hours, weeks, or months after the initial request for a sign.

The language of Spirit does not consist of full sentences; nor does it arrive in a perfect, orderly sequence of meaningful signs and events. Most times, we are required to piece together snippets of thoughts, dreams, signs, symbols, and moments of synchronicity in order to decode the meaning in the message.

Sometimes we hamper our ability to answer calls from the Afterlife because of preconceived ideas of how the message will arrive. What you expect will not always be what you get from the Afterlife. The language of Spirit is vast. Messages, signs and validations can come through in ways we least expect.

People who come to me for readings often question why their departed loved one has not given them a sign to say they're okay. When I ask, 'What were you expecting?' I get answers like, 'I thought the cupboard doors might fly open,' or, 'I thought I would see something like what happened in the movies *Ghost* or *The Sixth Sense*.'

Cupboard doors don't have to fly open; nor do you need to see an apparition or discover that your ornaments have mysteriously rearranged themselves to know that your departed loved one or Spirit has called.

When departed loved ones or Spirit decide to call, they *will* find a way to draw your attention. In my experience, spirit calls fall into three ringtone categories: synchronicity ringtones, dream ringtones, and natural wonder ringtones. But in saying that, no two people will sense a call in exactly the same way. Circumstances and experiences will always differ. Yet, when the call is recognised, it will create an incredible moment of validation.

Synchronicity's ringtone

Nothing happens by chance. So the next time you think something might be a coincidence – think again. It's likely to be Spirit calling as the next five amazing synchronicity ringtone encounters demonstrate.

Willie wagtail

Two years ago, Rachel came to me for a reading. Three years ago, she'd discovered she was adopted. Curious about her birth mother, Josephine, Rachel began a long and emotional search, which ended when Rachel found her mother's death certificate. Josephine died during childbirth, aged forty. Rachel felt a deep sense of guilt even though her mother's passing was not her fault.

Further to this, Rachel's research also revealed Josephine had never married. When Rachel asked a distant cousin on her mother's side who her father was, she shrugged and said, 'Who knows. I believe it was a holiday romance.' Rachel was shattered.

Needing closure, Rachel decided to drive to her mother's hometown. A local librarian remembered Josephine.

'She was quite smart and loved local history. We even have a copy of her unpublished journal in the library,' she offered.

On the way to the library, a sign pointing to a turn-off for the local cemetery caught Rachel's attention. Impulsively she diverted off the main road and headed toward the cemetery.

Despite the sky threatening rain, Rachel got out of her car and walked toward the headstones.

'I had no idea what I was doing, Mitchell, yet I felt driven,' explained Rachel.

In less than ten minutes, Rachel found her birth mother's grave. Sitting on top of the headstone was a willie wagtail. Rachel's presence didn't bother the willie wagtail in the slightest. He swished his tail and hopped from one place to another. His animated movements made Rachel laugh. 'Even though the first drops of rain had started to fall he kept swishing his tail in a funny little dance on my mother's grave,' she explained.

Forty minutes later, Rachel was in the

library seated at a private study booth. In front of her sat her mother's journal. She knew the moment she opened it her life would change forever. There would be no going back. Rachel took a deep breath and then opened the journal, choosing a page at random. Time slowed down, suspending Rachel in a haze of astonishment and disbelief. Within the page margin, Rachel's mother had drawn a cartoon-like sketch of a small bird – a willie wagtail. Next to it she had written, 'Born to make us smile and will always dance in the rain.'

What an amazing example of spirit-inspired synchronicity! Even so, I still had to validate the willie wagtail was a message from her mother. Rachel didn't realise it at the time, but she had detoured to the cemetery because she heard Spirit calling.

Spirit will often line up a chain of profound moments and events to help you in some way. For example, have you ever been missing your departed loved one only to have a photo of them tumble down from a dusty top shelf? Or have you ever been thinking of your departed loved one when a car passes with their name, initials, or birth year on the numberplate?

Licence to receive

Jamie came to see me not long after his best friend, Danny, had passed due to leukaemia. It was a tragic waste of a young man's life. He was only twenty-eight. Every month Jamie would have dinner with Danny's parents. They all figured Danny wouldn't mind if they celebrated his memory by drinking their way through his red wine collection. One night Jamie said to Danny's parents, 'You know I thought Danny would have given me a sign by now.'

Jamie felt sure Danny would give him a sign by messing with his collection of Van Morrison CDs. Danny was never a fan of Van Morrison. When Danny first passed, Jamie played Van Morrison repeatedly in the hope it would make Danny mad enough to find his way back from

Heaven to stop him.

One night, while driving home from Danny's parents' house, Jamie heard the tell-tale thud, thud, thud of a stereo system coming from a car in the lane next to him.

'It made me laugh,' explained Jamie. 'If Danny had been with me, he would have said something like, "Now that's the sort of music you play if you want to pull chicks."'

As the car with the boom box shot past Jamie, the numberplate read 'MaddX'. Danny's surname was Maddix. Jamie had given Danny the nickname Mad X. And Danny always signed off on Jamie's birthday cards with, *cheers from – MaddX*.

What an incredible sign of validation. Who would have ever thought a numberplate could offer so much comfort. I explained to Jamie that Danny probably had called many times, but Jamie hadn't answered because he was expecting Danny to mess with his Van Morrison CDs. Only when Jamie relaxed and let go of his expectations could Danny get through with one of what I knew would be many messages to come.

When Spirit steps in to help or comfort us, it is like magic. It fills us with hope and restores our faith; someone *is* watching over us and there *is* life after death.

When filming the television series *The One: The Search for Australia's Most Gifted Psychic*, which aired on Channel Seven in 2008, I was sitting in the back of a taxi heading out to location. It was early in the morning. I had my window wound down no more than three centimetres. For me, fresh air on my face in the morning is equivalent to the *must-have* cup of coffee. So with my face angled to collect all the fresh air I could inhale, I silently connected to my spirit guides. I asked Spirit to help me with the day ahead. Performing psychic readings on location and fitting in with the technical and timing limitations of a filming schedule is exhausting. I asked Spirit to send me a sign they were with me for the day.

As the traffic lights turned red and the taxi came to a stop, a tiny white downy feather floated in through the almost closed window and landed on my lap. That was all the validation I needed to know that my call to the Afterlife was answered.

Profound moments of synchronicity happen all the time. Spirit is always close by and ready to help with any aspect of your life, whether it be business, sport, family, love, relationships, finance, and health. But sometimes calls from the Afterlife are just to say hello – as Roxanne discovered.

Hello from beyond

My friend Roxanne experienced a unique moment of validation. Her 'hello' call came through a complete stranger.

Not so long ago, Roxanne arrived at a conference. When she sat down in her allotted seat, a young girl grabbed her attention to the point where she could not take her eyes off her. The young girl looked so much like her friend Ann, who had sadly passed twelve months earlier. Naturally, Roxanne just kept staring in disbelief. All sorts of emotions were racing through her mind. Feeling Roxanne's intense stare the girl shifted in her chair uncomfortably, turned toward Roxanne and gave her the 'Do I know you' look. Roxanne whispered, 'I'm so sorry for staring at you, but you're the spitting image of my girlfriend who passed recently.'

It was so surreal that Roxanne felt compelled to ask the young girl what her name was. The young girl replied, 'My name is Annaleise.'

'That's incredible because I called my girlfriend Annie.'

It was then the young girl shifted the lapel of her jacket to reveal her name tag. It read 'Annie'. Roxanne had no doubt it was a 'hello from the other side' call divinely sent from her much-loved and dearly departed friend, Ann.

Hearts and roses

For some of my clients, wakes can be as stressful as organising a wedding or engagement party. Will my dearly departed approve of the guest list, music, eulogy, food, and venue? Will friends, family, and relatives think I've done enough? Have I done enough?

Julianne, a friend of mine, lost her mother not all that long ago. She had organised the most beautiful wake. She'd turned her mother's art studio into a picture of Heaven on earth. She had covered the walls in drapes of white, flowing fabric. She adorned outdoor chairs with white fabric covers, securing each with a big silver bow at the back. A canopy of fairy lights created a ceiling of stars. Vanilla-scented candles gave off a calm aroma.

All around white roses stood in clear crystal vases – their brown stems and dark green leaves contrasting against the white backdrop. Julianne selected the best of her mother's paintings and displayed each on an easel. The effect added splashes of colour, reflecting her mother's colourful personality and irresistible charm.

On the lectern sat a vase of deep red roses along with her mother's framed photograph.

Julianne ensured her mother's favourite music was playing and her favourite savouries were on offer – along with her famous pink icing cupcakes. Friends, family and relatives could not compliment Julianne enough. Despite all the reassurances, Julianne was still worried. *Would Mum have liked it? Was she there to see it?*

Once the wake was over, Julianne found herself standing alone walking from easel to easel admiring her mother's paintings. She asked her mother to give her a sign that she approved of her 'send-off'. Nothing happened.

The next morning, Julianne unlocked her mother's studio. It was time to dismantle and clean up. When she approached the lectern, one rose within the vase caught her attention. All the petals had dropped off. When she looked down onto the white floor, the red rose petals had fallen into the perfect shape of a heart. Julianne's Afterlife call from her mum was most definitely a sign of love and appreciation – giving Julianne the utmost reassurance.

Have you ever been shopping in the supermarket and overheard a stranger's conversation that has given you the solution to a problem you've been dealing with? Sometimes messages come through someone else's words of inspiration, taken from a stranger's conversation as Kristy discovered.

Miracle messenger

Some time ago, Kristy came to see me for a reading. Life for her over the past eighteen months had been a roller-coaster ride. Four months after her mum passed, she moved to London for work. Not long after arriving in London, she met the most wonderful man. They found a place together and started life as a couple. Kristy was in love. No less than twelve weeks later, Kristy discovered the love of her life had a very mean streak. Early one morning, after a huge fight, Kristy ran out of the flat in tears.

'In my prayers I'd been asking Mum what to do,' Kristy explained. 'I was scared my boyfriend would suddenly become very violent.'

As Kristy walked, she tried to calm herself down. She pretended her mum was walking alongside her. Kristy told her mum how much she missed not being able to ring her and discuss things. Paying little attention to where she was placing her feet, Kristy stepped onto a hopscotch game drawn on the footpath in chalk. A little girl looked up at her and said, 'You shouldn't be here. Go home.' Kristy froze on the spot, looked down at the little girl and said, 'That's it. I'm packing my bags and going back to Australia, alone.' Kristy later told me moving back to Australia was the best thing she had ever done. She'd taken the job in London to run away from her grief and entered a relationship for the wrong reasons. How blessed was Kristy? The little girl acted as a miracle messenger. Through the little girl's words of innocence came the voice of Spirit.

Dream ringtones

Loved ones and Spirit don't always call using physical signs in our waking moments. Sometimes they slip into our dream world to deliver a message. Dreams are wonderful portals to the Spirit World and often occur between sleep and wakefulness.

There is no mistaking a spirit-inspired dream. The theme is clear, and the images and thoughts stay with you for hours or days afterwards. Sometimes, people and places appear so *real* it feels like you're actually there – as if experiencing the event firsthand – as the next four heartfelt encounters prove.

Snap

When I was a teenager, my departed Uncle Aram came to me in a dream. He stood waving a newspaper at me saying, 'The newspaper is going to take your picture tomorrow.' The next day the town was alive with a carnival atmosphere. Hundreds of people were out and about enjoying an array of vibrant cultural activities. My friend and I threaded our way through the crowd, soaking in all the fun as we headed toward the library. When we entered the library, an amazing display of origami cranes captured our attention. My friend was fascinated.

'A class starts in five minutes,' said the librarian, noticing our interest.

The next thing we knew we were upstairs making our own paper cranes. We were the only teenagers in a group of older women. 'The newspaper is running late,' said one woman, excited. I immediately told them about my dream. That started a huge conversation about dreams and premonitions. The journalist and photographer arrived and *snap* – there I was the next day with my photograph in the newspaper just like my dearly departed uncle said.

Waking in fright

Not long ago Judy came to me for a reading. Even before she sat down, I could tell she was distressed.

'Last night I had the most terrifying dream,' she said.

In Judy's dream, it was a pitch-black night. Broken down on the side of the road was a small black Mazda. The driver, a young woman, was struggling to push the car out of the way of approaching traffic. Tired and hungry, Judy's husband failed to notice the car until it was too late. His fully loaded truck swerved then careered out of control, before tipping over and sliding across the road in a shower of sparks. The cabin hit a power pole, killing Judy's husband instantly.

Judy woke up screaming then realised she'd fallen asleep on the couch. Thank goodness, it was only a dream. Or was it? The foreboding feeling did not leave her. Judy took several deep breaths. She looked at the clock – 10.30 p.m. A sense of dread began filling every cell in her body. Instinctively, she reached for her mobile phone and called her husband. Judy just wanted to hear his voice. He was on night shift driving his truck.

'Where are you?' she asked.

When he answered, Judy froze. Reality had just merged with her dream. 'Watch out for the black Mazda broken down in the left lane!' she yelled.

At that moment, her husband's mobile phone dropped out. The call disconnected. Judy tried to ring back. She could not get through. She dialled again, no answer.

She sat staring at her phone, numbed by fear. Ten agonising minutes ticked by. The landline phone rang. Judy's legs and hands trembled as she stood up and walked over to answer it.

'Hey babe,' said her husband's cheerful voice. 'How did you know about the car? If I'd still been travelling in the left lane I wouldn't be talking to you right now.'

How fortunate. Judy didn't shake off her sense of foreboding. Instead, she followed her instincts and called her husband to warn him.

Spirit messages are not always premonitions filled with warnings. Sometimes spirit messages show you *how* to take action and in *which* direction to go.

Hirudoid cream

A friend of mine, Kate, had a vivid dream about her dearly departed mother. In the dream, Kate's mother pointed to her badly bruised leg and asked Kate to leave a tube of Hirudoid cream on the kitchen table. Kate was slightly amused by the dream because she didn't realise the dearly departed could injure themselves.

When Kate told her brother about the dream, he insisted Kate follow their departed mother's request and leave a tube of Hirudoid cream on the kitchen table.

The next day Kate inspected the tube – then laughed at herself.

'How ridiculous was I?' she said. 'I actually felt disappointed because the next morning there were no signs the Hirudoid cream had been used.'

So despite all sense of reason, Kate decided to leave the tube of cream on the table for one more night.

The following afternoon her sister rang. Kate propped herself up on the kitchen bench and settled in for a long chat. Spotting the tube of Hirudoid cream Kate immediately told her sister about the dream.

'That's it!' shouted her sister, excited.

'What is?' asked Kate, confused.

'That's the name of the cream!'

A soccer ball had hit Kate's sister's husband

in the face. But for the life of her, she could not remember the name of the cream their mum always kept in the first-aid cabinet to stop bruising.

Any guidance from Spirit, whether it's life-saving or simply a helpful hint, is always a great comfort, but sometimes the message is simply to say hello from the other side.

Love – in the gift of a rose

When Trish arrived at my rooms for her appointment, she was not alone in her grief. My psychic eye could see her departed mother standing right by her side – deeply concerned about Trish.

The reading had hardly begun when Trish's mum came through and held her arms out to show me a bright red rose and said the word 'dream' repeatedly. It didn't take me long to realise Trish had been sent a dream ringtone. In her dream, Trish stood in a beautiful garden of vibrant pink, yellow, orange, and white roses.

As the dream continued, Trish saw herself sampling the perfume of an exquisite pink rose. As she inhaled a feeling of peace and love overwhelmed her. When she looked up she saw her mother standing on the other side of the rose bush.

'You can't be here,' she said. 'You're dead.'

Trish's mum just smiled and handed Trish a beautiful red rose.

Two weeks later and the dream almost forgotten, Trish stepped outside early one Sunday morning to collect the newspaper from the front lawn.

'When I looked into the rose garden, I was dumbfounded,' said Trish. 'My red rose bush was failing to thrive, yet on it was the most glorious single red rose.'

'What did it remind you of?' I asked.

'The red rose Mum gave me in my dream.'

I smiled. I explained to Trish that the red rose in her dream *was* the sign her mum was calling. The rose appearing in her garden was validation that her mum was happy and settled in the Afterlife. In that instant, I felt a huge shift take place. Trish was now certain her mum was still with her – albeit in spirit. Finally, Trish's healing had begun.

Natural wonder ringtones

Just as your departed loved ones and Spirit can use dreams to alert you to their call, so can they synchronise with nature. One of the most memorable examples I know is when Belinda was flying back to Melbourne after the sudden passing of her mother.

Grief-stricken, Belinda sat staring out the small window watching the plane's toy-like shadow race along the clouds. All the while she was thinking to herself, *Mum, give me a sign that you're okay.*

Minutes later, the most beautiful rainbow encircled the shadow of the plane. Belinda rubbed her eyes and then the window, thinking it was an optical illusion. But the rainbow was there for all to see. Bright happy colours formed a perfect circle around the plane's toy-like shadow as it raced along the clouds. Belinda cried silent tears of joy. She understood and gladly received the message – her mum was 'okay'.

Whenever I see a rainbow, I take a moment to marvel at its beauty and thank Spirit for sending me untiring love, protection, and divine guidance.

I have a friend who paints with the clouds. Whenever she's stuck for inspiration she steps into her garden and lies down on the lawn. Looking up at the sky, she lets her eyes drift with the clouds and her mind float. Soon words, thoughts, and ideas inspired by the shapes in the clouds drift into her mind. I tell her to cherish those ideas because they're spirit-inspired.

As incredible as it may be to experience joy at the sight of a beautiful rainbow or see creative ideas in the clouds, there is something even more miraculous. That is when Spirit synchronises with the natural behaviour of birds, animals, and insects to coincide with and deliver a profound message.

Not so long ago I zipped into the car park at the rear of my unit. All the time while driving home, I had been thinking about my dearly departed uncle. As I stepped out of my car, two brightly coloured butterflies appeared out of nowhere spiralling above my head. While marvelling at their striking coloured wings, I knew this was a message from my departed loved one. So I raised my hand and extended my index finger like a perch. *Both* butterflies landed on my finger at the same time. I was ecstatic.

Another friend of mine was facing a challenging time at work. He didn't know who amongst his colleagues he could trust. So he asked Spirit for some guidance. The next night, just before going to bed, something triggered the security light. He had a quick look out the window, thinking it was the cat. A strange shape on the back lawn caught his attention. He walked outside to investigate. My friend was dumbfounded. The strange shape turned out to be a barn owl – not local to the region.

Convinced the owl was a sign from Above my friend thumbed through reference books he owned on Native American symbolism. He discovered that the owl is a divine messenger associated with clairvoyance and the ability to foresee the future. When I asked my friend how he thought that applied to him, he said, 'Spirit is telling me to trust my own intuition with respect to what is happening at work.'

The next time your departed loved one's favourite song bursts onto the radio, your dog barks at photos, and birds appear at significant times – *know* that it is the Afterlife calling. Pick up and answer. Trust the moment of validation.

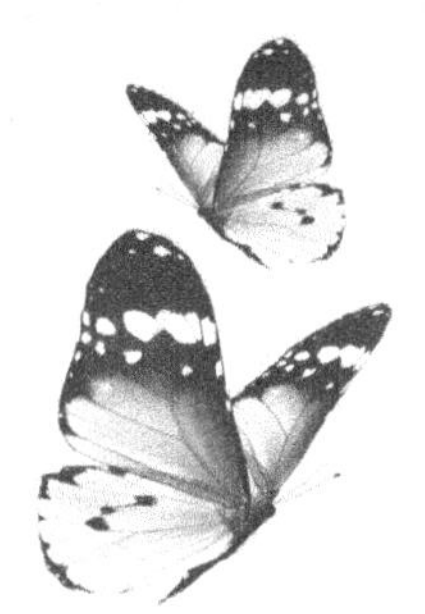

CHAPTER 7

PSYCHIC PROTECTION

The instant Kelly greeted her new client, Vivien, a cold shiver ran down her spine and goosebumps crept up her arms. Kelly responded by rubbing her arms warm as she ushered Vivien into the first of three beauty treatment rooms. After ensuring Vivien was warm and comfortable, Kelly began Vivien's massage. Minutes later Kelly excused herself, quickly exited the room, and burst into uncontrollable tears. 'Mitchell, it was so awful. The moment I began the massage, a strange feeling of tiredness overcame me that was followed by intense emotions of sadness and worthlessness.'

Kelly explained it was as if she were raking her finger through her client's darkest thoughts. Unfortunately, Kelly had unintentionally tapped into her client's innermost personal turmoil on a psychic level.

There is an invisible thread of psychic energy that links us to those we relate to on a daily basis. Just like air, psychic energy is an unseen force. Its effect can be clean and positive or toxic and negative. So I asked Kelly if she practised any form of psychic protection – especially before beginning her working day. Kelly paused then laughed nervously.

'But I don't do psychic readings like you, Mitchell. I only apply beauty treatments.'

I explained to Kelly some people store stale, negative, and toxic energy. They carry it with them until they find somewhere to dump it. Sadly, that 'somewhere' is usually on another person. Some people dump their energy intentionally while others have no idea they're doing it – like Kelly's client.

When we encounter negative energy it drains us. Perhaps you've already experienced it. Have you ever felt zapped of energy after being in the company of a friend, relative, or co-worker? Many report feeling 'dizzy' or 'light-headed' and 'spaced out'. These are classic symptoms. When another person drains our positive energy or dumps negative energy on us our body responds.

Have you arrived at a friend's house only to enter and immediately sense a dense cloud of angry energy hanging in the air? Without needing to ask, you know that an argument took place not long before you arrived. When I sense dense negativity in a room, I usually walk out again. Where possible, I prevent negative energy from attaching to me.

Many people intuitively sense negative

energy – especially when walking into a room or meeting someone for the first time. For example, a friend of mine is a real estate agent. Within seconds of walking into a newly listed home, she will sense whether the home gives off good or bad energy. Once when she was stuck with a bad energy home no one wanted to buy, I suggested she burn a sage stick before her next 'open for inspection' day. She laughed at me but tried it anyway. The house sold the next day.

Sadly, there are occasions where people come to me for a reading and I discover they are carrying dumped negative energy. I recall another client of mine. Even before Dianne sat down, I could see by her face that she was exhausted.

'I know I look tired,' she said, after catching my look of concern, 'but I'm just lacking in vitamins.'

Dianne didn't need to explain. I had already sensed a lack of vitamins was not her problem. What concerned me more was the cloud of negative energy surrounding her. The cloud was so dark and dense it had polluted her aura and lowered her energy vibration. To find out more, I asked if I could hold a piece of her jewellery. As soon as my fingers grasped Dianne's wristwatch, I felt a sharp pain in the back of my neck. Seconds later my mouth went dry and my pulse started racing. I felt someone plucking at my brain, confusing my thoughts. As I continued her reading, I sensed Dianne loved her work, yet it was making her anxious and nauseous. Not only that, Dianne usually left work with a splitting headache.

'Even my stomach feels hollow and empty at work – and that's after I've eaten,' she said.

Unfortunately, Dianne was under psychic attack. Each day her boss presented her with more work and tighter deadlines. To keep up, Dianne often stayed back late and worked on weekends – all for no extra pay. When she finally approached her boss and asked for help, he said no. In addition, Dianne's boss threatened that if she did not meet her deadlines three other people were waiting in the wings, all of them eager to step onto the stage and take her job. Dianne's boss was a psychic vampire and a bully. But it didn't stop there.

His attitude fostered unhealthy competition in the workplace. His 'win at all costs' motto created an environment loaded with feelings of rivalry, jealousy, and suspicion along with aggressive and uncooperative behaviour. Dianne's work environment was a toxic energy zone full of negative thought-forms.

Negative thought-forms

People are constantly broadcasting subtle energy vibrations just as we're constantly receiving them. For example, how many times has someone passed by you in the supermarket aisle and you've immediately thought, *Wow – she's really angry*, or, *He's a vibrant person*, or, *She's very calm*? Our spontaneous thoughts often identify the broadcasts we receive. Sometimes our bodies react as well. Many people subconsciously fold their arms as a way of shielding themselves from negative broadcasts.

During the average working day, you're likely to be surrounded by a mixture of people broadcasting positive and negative energy vibrations. Crucial to spiritual health is learning how to block negative broadcasts – especially those that emanate from jealous, competitive, tense, anxious, or stressed people. In Dianne's case, her wellbeing was not going to improve until she learnt to protect herself. She needed to master the art of turning her aura into a super shield.

A spiritual development circle in my hometown conducted an amazing experiment. The convener of the group took two clear drinking glasses. In each glass, he placed one orange. He labelled one glass orange A and the other

B. Once a week, the convener placed orange A in the middle of his development circle. The group focused thoughts of protection, love, and longevity onto orange A. Orange B, by comparison, was stored on a shelf where it sat open and receptive to all energy vibrations.

After four weeks, orange A remained perfectly fresh. Orange B, on the other hand, was rotting. And it wasn't just skin deep. When the convener sliced orange A in half, both halves were still juicy and sweet. Orange B, by contrast, was dry, pithy, and rotten inside. If positive thoughts projected on an orange can have that effect then imagine the impact negative broadcasts are having on you.

Crucial to any form of psychic work is psychic protection. Sometimes people forget or simply don't know how to protect themselves. There have even been instances where people who have left themselves open to all broadcasts have accidentally attracted dark energy from low vibration souls.

In my experience, low vibration souls are those who have not evolved. They choose not to learn from their physical life's lessons; nor do they aspire toward a level of purity and goodness. As a result, low vibration souls don't guide from within the Light like highly evolved souls. Instead, they prefer to exist in the shadows and manipulate from the dark. At times, low vibration souls can be deceptive, manipulative, and malicious – especially if that was their nature in life. Typically, low vibration souls are opportunists. They find it easy to tune into those who have left their aura open and exposed to all energy forms. However, there is no cause for alarm. There are many ways to apply a super shield coating to your aura.

In my early teens, I was sitting at Sydney's Central train station. I hadn't been there long when a Buddhist monk sat next to me. I smiled and said hello, noting how calm his energy felt. Much to my surprise, the Buddhist monk turned to me and asked if he could help me. I said yes, with no understanding of what he meant. Gently, the monk rose to his feet and turned to face me. He began rhythmically clapping his hands in a circular motion above my head and around my shoulders. As he did, a gentle hum resonated deep within his chest. Within seconds peace and calm had settled on me like a heavy early morning mist.

'What did you just do?' I asked when the monk had finished.

'I cleansed and protected your aura,' he replied with a smile.

I was so humbled by the experience 'thank you' didn't seem enough.

'One day you will return this energy to others tenfold,' he said.

To this day, I still use the handclapping technique to shift negative energy as demonstrated by the Buddhist monk.

Tools of protection

The tools of psychic protection I use and share with you here are easy and flexible. They can be adapted to suit your beliefs and lifestyle. For me, safeguarding my aura has become second nature, just like washing my hands before dinner.

Keep in mind you're not limited to using one technique at a time. You can mix and match. Explore the techniques until you find the perfect psychic protection combination for you.

Bubble of light

Before I leave home for the day, I spend five minutes protecting myself with purple and gold light – my favourite colours. I close my eyes and draw in a few deep breaths to still my mind. In my mind's eye, I imagine my body surrounded by a bubble filled with purple and gold light, but you can use whatever colours appeal to you. As

I inhale deeply, I imagine purple and gold light streaming into my aura. As I exhale slowly, I imagine the purple and gold light becoming a super shield – empowering my aura with the ability to deflect all negative energy. To close my bubble of light I thank Spirit for sending me divine protection.

If ever I feel the need for added protection, something I like to do is dab a drop of lavender oil on the back of my neck. The neck is one of the first places psychic attack occurs. Anytime you sense negative energy broadcasts, or you're exposed to energy zappers, psychic vampires, or energy dumpers, reapply the lavender oil.

Cutting cords

Sometimes, the energy broadcast from a certain situation, place, or person can tap into the life force of our very soul. When that happens, an invisible psychic tube – much like an umbilical cord – drains us of our energy reserves.

Have you ever experienced feeling drained

after being in the company of someone who complains constantly, talks about him or herself incessantly, or likes to argue every point? And have you noticed that every time you meet with or think about that person, you find yourself experiencing negative emotional or physical responses. Many of these responses include exhaustion, anxiousness, and feeling drained.

As part of my psychic hygiene and protection I routinely cut cords. Cutting negative psychic cords is easy and simple.

Close your eyes and sweep your hand around your body in a clockwise direction. As you do, imagine gathering any negative psychic cords into a bundle. Using your other hand, imagine taking a big pair of golden scissors and use them to cut the cords – severing any negative ties.

After cutting cords you may instantly feel lighter. Much like when a heavy weight is lifted off your shoulders.

Reflective mirrors

There may be times when you feel that you need additional help in protecting yourself from the people around you. This might be especially so when you're surrounded by complainers, pessimists, and energy dumpers. All you have to do is picture yourself in the centre of a ring of mirrors. With the reflective side facing out, the mirrors will deflect any negative broadcasts near you.

Saging

Native American Indians have long burnt white sage believing the sacred smoke dispels negative energy and clears troublesome spirits. You may know the technique by the name of 'saging' or 'smudging'. Today, sage smudge sticks are available from most new-age specialty stores. If you haven't seen one before, a sage smudge stick looks like a bundle of dried leaves bound together by a string.

For me, saging is a necessary part of my

spiritual house cleaning – just like vacuuming and washing the floors. Once I have my sage stick producing a healthy plume of smoke I walk around the room while circling the smudge stick in an anticlockwise direction. I even use my other hand to waft the sage smoke into corners, cupboards, and stairwells – any place where negative energy can linger or hide. Keep in mind that once negative energy shifts, it needs somewhere to escape. So make sure you leave windows and doors open while saging. That way fresh clean air can rush in to restore a positive balance.

Saging is an extremely powerful psychic protection and cleansing technique. You can use sage smoke to spiritually house clean, dispel low vibration energy, clear toxic energy, and protect yourself against psychic attack. I regularly circle sage smoke around my body, my reading room, and the inside of my home for this very reason. One friend of mine keeps a small drawstring pouch filled with dried white sage leaves in her handbag to act as a protective talisman. Another friend places a protective crystal in her sage pouch and hangs it on the inside door handle of her baby's room.

Not so long ago I had an opportunistic, low vibration soul slip through while I was performing a reading, live on radio. Fortunately, the soul was mischievous rather than 'evil' – but even so it caused problems. First, it tried to intimidate me with its strong cold presence. Despite goosebumps creeping up my left arm and shivers running down my spine, I stayed focused on the readings I was giving to callers. Not to be defeated, the presence caused my headphones to malfunction. Suddenly I could only hear fragments of words and sentences. Even so, I managed to hear enough to continue with the readings. The presence persisted. Next, it caused the computer managing incoming calls to malfunction. The last straw for me was when it started crossing the lines. I'd start a reading with one caller and end up with three others on the same line. That's when I signalled to the producer for a music break. Thankfully, I was carrying a sage smudge stick in my psychic toolkit. Shifting the low vibration energy was simple. Doing so without setting off the studio's smoke detector was the tricky part.

In addition to teaching me handclapping to shift energy, the Buddhist monk I met also kindly presented me with a miniature set of brass prayer bells. Like sage smoke, prayer bells raise the energy vibration within a room. Their ringing resonates at a frequency proven to drive out low vibration or toxic energy. I often ring my prayer bells before and after meditation.

Water

Water is a powerful conductor of energy. Many cultures, including those of ancient Rome, China, and Japan, have long used water as a therapeutic treatment. The ancient Greeks took therapeutic baths. The Native Americans included water in many of their healing systems. More recently, Dr Masaru Emoto demonstrated what the spiritual world has long known. Positive and negative energy affects the soul.

When Dr Emoto looked under a microscope at ice crystals formed from clean water exposed to loving words he discovered something amazing. The frozen water crystals had formed colourful and beautiful snowflake patterns. In contrast, ice crystals formed from polluted water exposed to negative words created dull, ugly, and asymmetrical patterns. Given the human body is approximately sixty-five per cent water it makes sense that what we do, what we say, and how we feel affects every cell in our body.

You can harness the protective power of water by writing the words 'wellbeing', 'balance', and 'harmony' onto a strip of paper. Next, tape your wellbeing power words onto your water bottle. Some people prefer to drop a healing crystal into the water instead of using words. Either way, leave the bottle standing overnight in the fridge. In the morning, pour yourself a glass of water. Drink only from that bottle of water for the rest of the day. With each sip, know that Spirit has infused the water with the protective energy you requested along with a little extra divine love. This healing gift from Spirit will help boost your aura and protect you from forces that drain your energy.

If restless nights are causing you to wake feeling tired, I recommend a technique used by many, including myself. Try placing a bowl or glass of water near your bed. The water will protect you by attracting and absorbing negative energy. Sometimes, you may even see tiny bubbles of trapped negative energy on the inside of the glass or bowl. *Never* drink or feed the water that has trapped dense negative energy to plant life or animals.

Did you realise showering can fast-track negative energy absorption? Running water dissolves and neutralises negative energy. Just recently *Spirit and Destiny* magazine published a survey by shower manufacturer Mira. According to their survey, over sixty-four percent of British people take a shower to improve their mood or de-stress after work. I know it works for me. What about you?

If you're lucky like me and live near the beach, diving into cool ocean waters can also fast track the cleansing and neutralising of stored negative energy.

Crystal power

Special, extraordinary, and magical – these properties have been associated with crystals since ancient times. Today, professional crystal therapists report crystal healing contributes to profound improvements in health and spiritual wellbeing.

Anyone can use crystals to restore harmony and balance. Some of my personal favourite protective stones include a combination of black tourmaline, amethyst, and smoky quartz. Each stone possesses a high vibration frequency that forms a natural barrier against low vibration and toxic negative energies. The easiest way to harness the protective power of crystals is to carry or wear them. Whenever I wear crystals, I like to make sure as much of the crystal as possible is in contact with my skin. Crystals convey their high vibration energy far more efficiently when in direct contact with the body

When using crystals, it is important to cleanse them regularly. The simplest method is to wash your crystals under running water. Likc taking a shower, the water neutralises and dissolves any negative energy stored in the crystal. Some people prefer to bathe their crystals in saltwater. Others purify them using moonlight. The choice is yours.

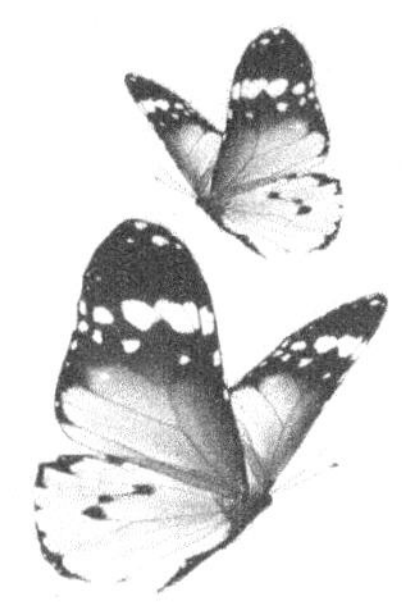

CHAPTER 8

DIALLING SPIRIT

We can all dial the Afterlife. There is no secret number, silent code, or password to remember. You don't even need a special phone. All you need is an open mind, a technique to align your energy with Spirit and a question from the heart.

Recently, during one of my psychic development workshops, I was teaching Angela the skill of automatic writing – one of the many wonderful ways you can train yourself to connect with Spirit intuitively.

'What's wrong?' I asked, when I noticed Angela had filled the page with circles. 'I don't know, Mitchell. I must be doing something wrong.'

I explained to Angela that Spirit was most likely trying to align its energy vibration with hers – a bit like tuning a guitar. Only after you've found the correct tension will each guitar string produce the right note. Spirit has to adjust its frequency in order to vibrate in harmony with you. Until Spirit finds your note, all you may receive is out-of-tune lines, squiggles, and circles. However, I sensed a deeper issue was troubling Angela – one that was blocking her ability to react spontaneously and intuitively.

'What is it that you truly seek from Spirit?' I asked.

During the lunch break, Angela opted not to join the others in her group. Instead, she sat alone under a shady tree with her sketchpad and coloured pencils. In a dreamy state, she let her mind drift, recalling my words – *what is it that you truly seek from Spirit?*

Twenty minutes later, Angela held a drawing at arm's length. Something about the rocky cliff top overlooking a peaceful bay she had drawn filled her with a sense of familiarity. It was then Angela raced up to me as if she had solved one of the greatest mysteries of the universe.

'Look, Mitchell,' she said, placing her drawing down on the table in front of me. 'I was focusing on words. I was meant to draw a picture.

'Mum used to take me here when I was little. She loved to watch the sea eagles soar high above the bay ... *protecting us*, as Mum used to say.'

What Angela was truly seeking from Spirit was the answer to a question that had been troubling her for some time, 'What should I do with Mum's ashes?' Her drawing was the answer.

In my experience, no matter what technique you use to dial the Afterlife, Spirit will always find wonderful ways to answer your call. Often the answers will arrive in ways least expected.

Automatic writing

Have you heard of the author, journalist, and renowned psychic Ruth Montgomery? She claimed automatic writing contributed to her success. At the exact same time every morning, Ruth would sit at her writing desk. With her fingers poised on her typewriter keys, she'd wait for her guides to come through with stories and messages. The late Enid Blyton, children's author, also claimed her stories and characters were Spirit-inspired. The secret to both Ruth and Enid's automatic writing success rested with the individual techniques they used to dial Spirit and the questions they asked.

Generally, Spirit answers by tuning in with

your vibration and guides the writing (or drawing) tool. What happens after that can vary. Some people only produce scribble the first time they try. Other people draw pictures that range from full-scale masterpieces to child-like stick figures. Many remain unaware of what they are writing until the flow of inspirational communication stops. Some don't even recognise the resulting handwriting.

On my first attempt, I focused too hard on the pen in my hand. Success came when I relaxed and let my mind drift. Even so, I only drew circles the first few times. If this happens to you, it might be a sign Spirit is still getting used to communicating using a human vibration frequency. The telltale sign for me that Spirit was coming through was when my hand began to feel light and airy – as if the pen was no longer touching the paper.

Do you have a pressing question like Angela? Perhaps your question is entirely different. 'Should I buy this house?' or 'Should

I change jobs?' – as long as your question is specific and it comes from the heart, Spirit will do everything in its divine power to answer. However, it's important to remember Spirit will only answer in accordance with your divine soul print. For instance, if it's not within your destiny to win the lottery, Spirit is unlikely to come through with the winning numbers.

Once your question is decided, make sure you have a notebook and pens at the ready. Find your favourite quiet spot – one that radiates peace, harmony, and rejuvenation. For some people, that translates to a place with glorious ocean views. For others, returning to nature and sitting in the forest represents tranquillity. Many find a little piece of Heaven in their own garden. No matter where you sit, make sure your notebook is resting on a firm surface and your writing arm can move freely.

Before you begin, it's a good idea to apply a psychic protection technique you feel comfortable with. That way you can be open and receptive to Spirit while shielding yourself from any negative energy broadcasts near you.

When you're ready, open your notebook. Have your pen poised to write. Quiet your mind and relax your body. Close your eyes. Take several deep breaths. Each time you inhale, focus on asking Spirit your question. And each time you exhale, ask Spirit to come through with the answer. Even though you may not feel any different, trust Spirit is there to guide you.

Slowly open your eyes. Write your question at the top of the page in your notebook. It doesn't have to be a pressing question. It can be as simple as, 'Should I travel overseas?' 'Should I change jobs?' or, 'What do I need to know to keep moving forward?'

Continue to calm and relax your mind while focusing on your question. Observe your visions and thoughts. What can you *see*? Can you *hear* snippets of words or voices? Is there a familiar fragrance in the air? What colours appear? Write down everything you can see, hear, taste, and smell. Use single words or simple phrases. That way you are less likely to interrupt your psychic sensory flow.

Open your eyes. Look at the page or pages of automatic writing in front of you. It's important to silence your critical mind before it begins. It doesn't matter if the words you've written seem to be nonsense, or that the writing is untidy or all over the page. Instead, note the words and phrases that leap off the page at you. Ask yourself, 'How do these words answer my question?'

Try to repeat the exercise at the same time three or more days a week. Don't be surprised if you also experience spontaneous automatic writing episodes.

Twelve months ago, Kaleen lost her mother. While sitting in her living room alone, Kaleen had the sudden urge to pick up a pen and paper. Although she'd never studied calligraphy she drew the most beautiful and artistic letter K. Two days later, Kaleen was helping her dad sort through her mother's belongings. When she walked past the corkboard in the kitchen, a scrap of art paper caught her attention. It was sticking out from under a wad of bills pinned to the board. To Kaleen's astonishment, drawn on the piece of paper was the exact letter K she'd drawn two days earlier. When she later compared the two, the only difference was her mother's handwritten inscription that read 'To Kaleen – with love'.

Keep searching for meaning in your notes. It may not be until days or weeks later that your collection of drawings and keywords makes sense.

Successful automatic writing requires you to ask specific questions, relax, and allow the inspirational guidance to flow to you. With practice, you'll soon learn to write and understand the language of Spirit.

Dialling a dream

We are closest to the Spirit World when we are asleep. I sense this is so because our mind is most relaxed when we're asleep. No longer does our mind churn over the concerns of the waking day. For that reason, many of my clients and friends have had great success with spirit-inspired dreams.

For instance, just before writing this chapter, Mary sent me an email to thank me for teaching her how to dial a spirit-inspired dream. For months, Mary had been lying awake at night worrying about her 24-year-old son's reckless driving. She even tried pleading with him to sell his high-powered car, but her words fell on deaf ears. Mary knew her son was a danger to himself and others on the road. He'd already had several speeding fines and two accidents sustaining minor injuries.

For several consecutive nights, Mary dialled Spirit and prayed for a dream that would show her how to protect her son from his own reckless behaviour. Yet each morning she'd wake with no recollection of having had a spirit-inspired dream. Finally, Mary gave up asking, but two weeks later Spirit answered.

Mary's son was sitting at the breakfast table looking rather glum. When Mary asked, 'What's wrong?' her son answered, 'I think I'll sell my car.'

Mary almost choked on her cup of tea.

'I'm going to die in that car if I don't sell it,' he continued.

'What makes you think that?' asked Mary.

'Every night this week I've had the same nightmare. I lose control of my car and I slam head-on into a post on the side of the road and die.'

Mary's son was so convinced his dream was a premonition he traded his high-powered V8 car for a four-wheel drive. Mary was so relieved she bought him a membership to a four-wheel drive club. At least that way he'd learn how to pit his driving skill against the forces of nature without destroying himself, the environment, or anyone else.

Dialling a spirit-inspired dream is easy. However, there are no guarantees. Spirit may respond in ways you least expect – as Mary experienced.

You will need a notebook, pen and amethyst crystal. First, settle yourself into bed and open your notebook. Write your question at the top of a fresh page. Close your notebook but keep your question foremost in your mind. Just as in the automatic writing exercises, questions must be from the heart. Place the amethyst crystal under your pillow or on your bedside table. Amethyst protects you against negative energy by promoting peace, spiritual wisdom, and psychic abilities.

The moment sleep begins to rush over you like an incoming tide, repeat your dream question softly – just as a mother would sing a lullaby to a child. Upon waking, reach for your notebook. Record your immediate thoughts and impressions. Even if you think the information doesn't make sense – write down every detail. Use keywords and simple phrases to describe the images, ideas, emotions, sounds, and sensations you recall from your dream. Avoid writing full sentences. To do so will draw your thoughts to the process of writing instead of responding to the inspirational flow.

Sometimes there can be three or four elements to a spirit-inspired dream. These elements are like jigsaw pieces. Individually, the pieces may not make much sense, but when you put them together, they complete a picture. Dream books may even help further decode the symbols in your dreams.

Some people are lucky and receive answers within the first few nights. Don't be disappointed if you're not among them. Keep persisting. Even if your mind appears blank in the morning – keep trying. The language of Spirit does not develop overnight. It takes time for

Spirit to attune to your soul's dream vibration energy.

If you haven't had a breakthrough after several nights, put the exercise aside for a while. The chances are you're trying too hard or Spirit is attempting to answer you in another way. Remember, answers can arrive how you least expect. For example, have you ever dialled a girlfriend's number only to be surprised to hear an unfamiliar male voice answering the phone? Spirit can work much like that in your dreams too. The symbols and images are unfamiliar so you don't understand the message – just like you don't recognise the strange male voice on the phone.

Luke, a client of mine, was giving serious thought to buying a hobby farm. As so often happens, synchronicity was at play. A friend phoned and mentioned a road sign he'd seen advertising new hobby farm allotments. Luke rang the real estate agent later that day. While the price was right, Luke was unfamiliar with the location and the history of the land.

Luke decided to dial a dream requesting his recently departed father – who was an environmental scientist – for advice about what to do. Several nights went by. Not one spirit-inspired word, thought, or idea passed through his dreams. Then on the morning Luke was due to meet with the real estate agent, he decided to stop for a coffee. While waiting for his latte, Luke's ears pricked up when he heard two famer-types talking.

'Don't know how they managed to release that land for hobby farms,' commented one.

'No,' said the other. 'I remember that land as a kid. They used it for potato farming. I reckon it's still full of toxic Dieldrin residue.'

There was Luke's answer – divinely packaged in the words of two strangers who weren't even talking to him.

Both Mary and Luke's experiences demonstrate the divine wisdom of Spirit. Spirit could have complied with Luke's request to have his dad answer his question in a dream. But would Luke have understood the message as clearly? I sense not. The wiser and more appropriate response was to manipulate events to place Luke in the right place at the right time. Overhearing the two strangers talking left Luke with no doubt that he should decline the offer.

Synchronicity and divine timing play a huge role in the way Spirit answers us. Spirit will always choose the wisest and most appropriate means to answer questions. Even when we ask a question for which the timing is not right to receive an answer, Spirit applies divine wisdom. Quite often Spirit will leave clues – each one designed to place us in a better position for when the time is right to receive the answer in full.

Spiritual prayer box

Another wonderful way to dial Spirit and help others is to create a spiritual prayer box. Start by choosing a gorgeous box (shoebox size or smaller is ideal). Most craft stores sell pre-made boxes. Express your artistic soul – decorate your own. Some people even include words like trust, love, and eternity in their designs. If you don't have the luxury of spare time, visit your local newsagent or discount variety store. Choose a box from the fun range of decorated gift boxes found in store.

Once you have your spiritual prayer box, place it somewhere in your home that is sacred to you. To dial a spirit prayer for someone you love – living or passed – write his or her name on a piece of paper. Next to the name, write your wish. For example, Aunty Flow – may you find happiness in the Afterlife; Judy, my best friend – may you be blessed with amazing exam results; and Edna, my dear old neighbour – may your broken leg heal soon. You can even write one for yourself.

Once your wish is complete, place it inside the box. I often create prayers for healing, happiness, prosperity, peace, courage, faith, and love. Spirit is always listening and willing to help those in need.

Once a day, hold the spiritual prayer box in your hands. Close your eyes and focus your energy on the prayer box. Forward all your messages to Spirit and ask that your special prayers be answered in the wisest and most wonderful way.

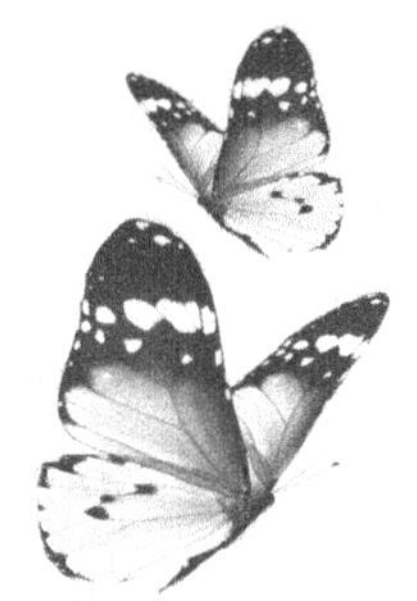

CHAPTER 9

PSYCHIC SENSING: FINETUNING THE SENSES

Can you remember a time when you had a hunch and trusted it because it felt right? Or perhaps you took a course of action that placed you in the right place at the right time to take advantage of a perfect opportunity. Maybe you've even experienced waking one morning with a sense of foreboding, 'knowing' that something bad was going to happen – and it did. These are what I call 'psychic moments'. Sadly, too many people dismiss such moments as lucky guesses or coincidences. They are not. Psychic moments validate that you are in tune with yourself, Spirit, and the universe around you.

The question is, what lies beyond a psychic moment? What force is at work? What makes you pick up your mobile phone just before it rings? How is it you know who is calling before you answer? Some call it a hunch, gut instinct, or a sixth sense. I call it 'psychic sensing'. Psychic moments happen because of your ability to pick up information psychically.

I believe everyone is psychic. To what degree depends on how 'tuned in' you are to the energy vibrations around you. In some ways, psychic ability is not unlike mobile phone reception. Some people are in close range and receive a full signal. Meanwhile, other people are further away and have a weaker signal that drops in and out. Even so, everyone can learn to strengthen their psychic powers and bring untold benefits into their life.

One question I always ask participants in my workshops is, 'If you were about to be stranded on an island with no power, shelter, shops or running water – and you could take up to three items with you, what would those three items be?' In the past I've received responses like, 'I'd take my mp3 player for music,' 'matches to light a fire,' 'a torch to light my way at night,' 'chocolate for energy,' 'food for sustainability,' 'blankets for warmth,' and 'lots of rope to bind a shelter together'. When participants ask me what I would take I answer, 'My instinct.'

If you strip away every comfort and push human beings to the limit to survive, natural instinct kicks in. After all, natural instinct kept primitive man alive. In the modern world, our natural instinct manifests as intuition. That's why I say everyone has a degree of psychic ability because intuition has been a natural energy present from birth since the dawn of man.

Sometimes you may find other people are the first ones to notice your natural psychic ability. Perhaps you've been at the receiving end of comments like, 'You were so right about the guy I met last night. How did you know?' 'Why were you so sure I would be offered the job when there were over one hundred other applicants?'

Sometimes people don't pay as much attention to their own thoughts and reactions as their friends do. Do you solve problems in your dreams? Do you experience 'a-ha' moments while taking a shower? Do strong sensations like 'butterflies in the stomach' or 'hairs standing up on the back of your neck' influence your judgment concerning people or situations? Does an 'inner voice' guide the decisions you make? If you answered yes to most of these questions then it is highly likely you are among those who have been psychic sensing and receiving divine guidance, perhaps without even realising it.

Your psychic sensing may come naturally in the form of feelings, inspired thoughts, dreams, symbols and pictures. Or you may need gentle coaching before you can unleash your true psychic potential.

There are three major psychic senses. They are psychic seeing, psychic feeling, and psychic hearing. How you unleash your psychic senses depends on your sensory preferences. Everyone is different. Visual people tend to 'see' while deep thinkers who mull over things tend to 'feel'. Those who are active and chatty often 'hear'. Identifying your primary psychic sense is the best way to discover where your psychic strengths lie. Everyone has at least one primary psychic sense they can develop. You may find you're strongly gifted in two or all three.

Psychic seeing

Are you someone who routinely forecasts outcomes? Do you often hear yourself starting a sentence with, 'I can see ...' For example, 'I can see you stepping on glass if you don't wear the right hiking boots,' or, 'I can see your cake decorating class is going to lead you into starting your own business,' or, 'I can see if you don't make that call now you'll miss speaking with him altogether.' People with the skill of psychic seeing have a phenomenal ability to highlight milestones like events, incidences, special occasions, and daily occurrences before they happen.

Perhaps you often catch glimpses of movement out of the corner of your eye, yet when you turn to look no one is there. Or are you someone who sees the brief appearance of coloured mist or flashes of darting lights? Maybe you've even experienced an object catching your attention, but when you take a closer look it's gone.

If so, did you rub your eyes and take a second look?

Maybe you have dreams so vivid they seem real. If so, do events in those dreams unfold with such clarity that you wake remembering every single detail? Or is daydreaming more your style? Do you enjoy letting your mind drift? Have you ever seen snapshots of scenes, signs or symbols that foretell of future events but you don't realise until they unfold hours or days later?

If you nodded your head, or answered 'yes' or 'sometimes' to any of the experiences I've just described, then it's likely your dominant sense is *seeing*. For you, Spirit has a dazzling way of slipping messages into your dreams or waking hours in the form of visions, sightings, symbols, and snapshots.

To further develop psychic seeing, spend a few minutes every day opening your 'spiritual eyes'.

Close your eyes. Turn in a clockwise

direction three times and then turn anticlockwise three times. Do you still know which way you are facing? The idea while doing this exercise is to practise seeing through your closed eyelids. Using your mind's eye, try and 'see' all the things in the room as you turn clockwise then anticlockwise.

Before opening your eyes, tell yourself which way you are facing in the room and what items will be in front of you. Afterwards, open your eyes and note your accuracy.

When encouraging your spiritual eyes to open you can gently circle your index finger over your 'third eye'. (Your third eye is the area on your forehead between your eyebrows.) Visualise a purple lotus flower opening to display its petals in full bloom. This to me symbolises my spiritual eyes are open. Persevere with this exercise. Given time, you'll soon tone your psychic muscle and strengthen your natural skills of psychic seeing.

Psychic feeling

Butterflies in the stomach and hairs rising on the back of the neck are just two of the many physical signs that can indicate the sense 'psychic feeling' is in play.

People with psychic feeling as their dominant sense often report their hands 'warm up' or 'tingle' when certain emotions are being broadcast by individuals near them. Some even say shaking hands can be like looking into a person's heart. The handshake enables them to 'feel' the true state of that person's emotions. Walking into a crowded room or walking down an unfamiliar street can produce the same result for psychic feeling people. They instantly get a 'good' or a 'bad' feeling. They know whether to tread with caution or relax and enjoy.

If you know someone who is sensitive in this way it's likely you'll hear them qualify what they're about to say with, 'I feel ...' For example, 'I feel I can trust this person,' or, 'I feel trouble brewing ...' or, 'I feel that person is very happy, but is putting on a stern face.'

One simple way to stimulate your psychic feeling is to rub the palms of your hands together in a circular motion. After thirty seconds, slowly move your palms away from each other until they're about a ruler length apart. Now bring your focus to the space between your palms. Can you 'feel' that space?

Slowly bring your palms toward each other again. Continue to focus on the space between your palms. Does the intensity of the energy you feel in the space vary depending on how far apart your palms are? In the past, participants in my workshops have made varying comments like, 'Wow, my energy is the size of a golf ball,' all the way through to, 'The energy I sense between my hands is the width of an invisible basketball'.

Before a psychometric reading or when holding a photograph, I rub my hands together to activate my psychic energy. I do this because I receive psychic impressions whenever I hold objects in my hand.

Often those with a powerful sense of touch become healers. A good healer can literally improve a person's physical, emotional, and spiritual wellbeing with their bare hands. The divine healing energy channelled through the practitioner's hands alters the energy surrounding the client, which helps to restore energy, balance, and offers a sense of rejuvenation.

Psychic hearing

Psychic hearing is not just limited to hearing spirit voices and noises. Many report they hear sounds from the future. Either sounds that come from inside their head or as though they are outside. Perhaps you're among such people. Have you ever run to answer the phone only to discover it's not ringing when you reach it? Yet, when you turn to walk away, it rings.

How many times have you been singing along to a tune in your head only to turn on the radio and hear the exact same song playing? When that happens to me, I'm usually synchronised to within one or two words.

In some instances, people have been so in tune with their psychic hearing Spirit has been able to shout, 'Duck,' 'Run,' 'Look out,' or, 'Slow down,' in order to save their life. Yet when the danger passed and people in these situations turned to thank their saviour, they discovered they were alone. Another example I often give in workshops is of a three-year-old toddler who hears a voice yell, 'Don't touch that!' At that point, the toddler is reaching up on his tippy toes to grab a pot handle sticking out over the cooktop. When he turns around to see who is watching he realises he's alone. So he gives grabbing the pot handle another shot. At that moment, his mum walks back into the kitchen just in time to scoop him up in her arms and whisk him out of harm's way.

When psychic hearing is your dominant sense, you're capable of listening to another level of vibration, making it possible to hear spirit noises and possibly voices. When your psychic hearing is in tune you will hear things others won't – much like when a dog hears a dog whistle, yet its owner can't.

To strengthen your psychic hearing, try training yourself to hear beyond normal boundaries. You can do this by holding your right hand over your right ear and listening intently with your left ear. Try to stretch the hearing in your left ear as far as it will go. It might even help to do this outside. For example, you might feel your hearing stretches as far as the tall pine trees three blocks away. After thirty seconds, remove your hand from your right ear. Can you feel how far the hearing in your right ear stretches in order to balance with your left ear?

Once your hearing balances itself again, repeat the same exercise but with opposite ears. So cover your left ear with your left hand

and stretch your hearing as far as you can with your right ear.

Now try covering both ears for thirty seconds and then take your hands away. How far did your hearing extend that time? Some people find one ear is stronger than their other ear. Spirit usually talks to me using my right ear.

Given time and practice, single words followed by short phrases, sounds, and music may even float past your psychic ear.

Finetuning the senses

I'm constantly finetuning my psychic senses of seeing, feeling, and hearing. You can do this too. For instance, while writing out my shopping list I make a note at the top of the list of three fruits I sense will be on sale. When I get to the supermarket, I dash to the fruit and veggie section to check if I'm right.

While travelling to the supermarket I visualise a free parking space close to where I want to be. Sometimes I even visualise the colour of the car that will reverse out of *my* parking space just as I arrive.

When the phone rings, I practise tuning into identify the caller before I pick up or look at the caller ID on the screen.

A good friend of mine meets with her friends at a busy café every Saturday morning. While waiting for everyone to arrive she practises stretching her hearing to as many tables away from her right ear and then her left as she can.

You'll hardly notice you're exercising your 'psychic muscle' when you incorporate finetuning your psychic senses with your daily activities. But let me warn you, the rewards may astound you.

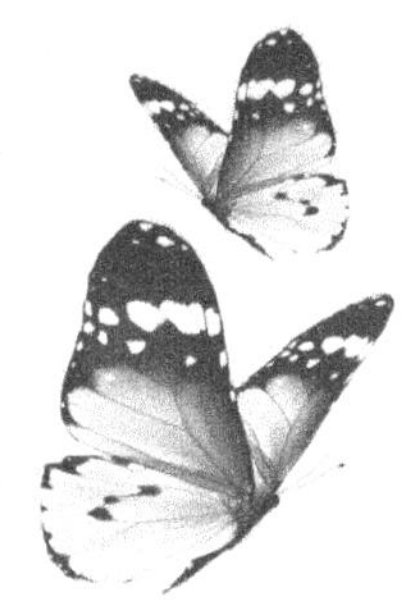

CHAPTER 10

SENSING THE NEED: SEEKING A PSYCHIC MEDIUM

If only I knew Dad was happy in the Spirit World. *If only* I knew Mum passed peacefully. *If only* I knew what the future had in store for me. 'If only ...' is a potent indicator that a powerhouse of mixed emotions is generating unrest deep within our soul. And when 'if only' is followed by a question concerning a departed loved one, a relationship, or a life-changing decision it sends most people into a frantic, if not desperate, search for answers.

Today, people from all walks of life consult psychics when in search of answers. Over the years, my clientele has included a wide range of fascinating people. I've read for celebrities nervous about their future, mums concerned about the destiny of a particular child, and high-profile entrepreneurs faced with making multimillion dollar decisions. I've even read for other psychics. Rich and famous, business entrepreneur or a fabulous mum at home – we're the same when it comes to searching for answers about the past, present, and future. So how do you choose a good psychic?

Selecting a psychic is no different to choosing any other professional service. I know when I choose a doctor, dentist, or hairdresser I ask my friends and family for recommendations. I find word-of-mouth referrals are often the best. So ask others if they know of a good psychic medium they can recommend. Find out what methods the psychic used. Did they use tarot cards, hold onto jewellery, or ask for a photograph? Are they a straight shooter or do they take the softly-softly approach? Questions like these can help you to determine if you'll like the psychic's personal style of reading. Always trust your intuition.

Sadly, psychics can't be all things to all people. Many psychics specialise in reading the present and the future while others may delve into past lives. Mediums, on the other hand, have the rare ability to communicate with departed loved ones. However, did you realise that while all mediums are psychic, not all psychics are mediums?

Pru was feeling grief-stricken and directionless. Three weeks ago, she dropped everything and flew home from London. Her mother had passed suddenly. Sadly, Pru didn't get a chance to say goodbye and consequently felt a deep sense of guilt and regret.

Early one Saturday afternoon, Pru was in

the supermarket grocery shopping. By chance, she ran into her old friend who had just been to see a psychic who read tarot cards.

'It was so uplifting, insightful, and empowering,' raved Pru's friend. 'You should go.'

Convinced it was a sign from Above, Pru booked an appointment with the same psychic.

But, by the end of the session, Pru felt disappointed. Pru had pinned her hopes on making a connection with her recently departed mother. She badly needed to say sorry to her mother for not being by her side when she passed. Unfortunately, Pru did not realise that not all psychics are mediums. A wiser choice, in Pru's case, would have been to consult a psychic medium – someone who could tap into the Spirit World and read the future.

The secret to a satisfying reading is making sure you match the psychic skill with your most pressing questions. I suggest you create a list of five questions you most want answered during the reading. This will help you to determine the spiritual advisor most suited to answering your questions. If most of your questions relate to a departed loved one then choose a medium or psychic medium. But if most of your questions relate to your future, finance, work, or a major life-changing decision then perhaps a psychic medium or even a tarot card reader may be a more appropriate choice. Your questions may relate to gaining a better understanding of yourself or the longevity of a relationship with a husband, partner, or lover. While a good psychic medium may be able to give you a good insight into questions of this nature, an astrologer or numerologist will be able to chart compatibility and provide a long-range forecast.

Tools of the psychic trade

Not all psychics sense and connect with Spirit in the same way. Some use tarot cards, read palms, or consult a crystal ball. Some may even look into your teacup to reveal your destiny while others prefer to hold onto a personal object or consult predictive systems like astrology and numerology. Other spiritual intuitives may use no tools at all. They can tap into the past, present, and future by simply looking at you.

I'm a clairvoyant, clairsentient, and clairaudient psychic medium. That means I see, hear, and feel information passed on to me from the Spirit World and departed loved ones. So when clients arrive for their appointment I offer them the choice of connectng with someone special in the Spirit World or focusing on their future. My spiritual gifts enable me to focus on the past, present and future aspects of a person's life as well as receiving messages from their departed loved ones and spirit guides. Determining what aspect my client would like me to focus on is important because it influences the psychic tools and techniques I use.

Palmistry

Palmistry is an ancient art still in practice

today. By looking at the formation of certain lines and mounts on the palm of your hand, a good palmist can interpret many aspects of your life.

Most palmists begin by examining both hands. With a right-handed person, the left hand is the 'birth hand'. It indicates the person's character. The right hand reflects individuality, flexibility, and potential. (The opposite hands apply for left-handed people.)

While I don't read palms per se, they do 'talk' to me. Sometimes I'll ask clients to place their hands on the table, palms facing upwards. When I touch the client's palms, information transfers to my third eye – just as if the palms are talking to me.

Some palmists even examine the characteristics of the fingers, fingernails, fingerprints, and skin patterns. The shape of the hand along with flexibility also plays an important role. For example, a *square hand* identifies the practical person, someone forceful, purposeful, and capable of achieving success. A *tapering hand* is likely to belong to an artist, joyous, enthusiastic, and a sensitive soul. A *spade-like hand* denotes an energetic owner with positive actions. A *pointed hand* belongs to an idealist, and a *long hand*, with knot-like joints, belongs to a thinker or philosopher. Moderate flexibility in the hand tells of an easygoing personality, while great flexibility indicates a freethinker. Stiffness suggests stubbornness.

It's important to understand that while palmists can predict when you'll get married and how many children you'll have, it is unlikely they will be able to describe your future husband. Palmists can plot your timeline from birth to death – indicating major life events along the way.

What I also find amazing is that the lines on the palm of our hands change over time and in accordance with our life experiences. All of which supports we really do hold our destiny in the palm of our hands.

Tarot cards

The tarot is a deck of seventy-eight cards divided into two sections. These are the Major Arcana, which consists of twenty-two cards, and the Minor Arcana, which has fifty-six cards. Cards drawn from the Major Arcana tell the story of our journey through life and some of the challenges we're likely to encounter along the way. Illustrations on the Major Arcana generally depict each card's meaning, but not always.

The Minor Arcana is divided into four suits – Cups, Wands, Swords, and Pentacles. There are fourteen cards in each suit. The Minor Arcana deals with the detailed situations we meet in our life such as relationships, prosperity, loss, fulfilment, and life-changing decisions.

Generally, tarot readers ask you to shuffle the deck of cards. After which you choose a number of cards from the deck. The tarot reader then lays the selected cards out on a table to form a specific spread or pattern. While my clients are shuffling the tarot cards, I ask them to focus their energy on the questions they would like answered.

Where the cards fall and how they relate to each other within the spread indicates past events, current surrounding influences, and the future. In my experience, consulting tarot cards can prove to be very accurate.

Generally, my psychic readings don't begin with tarot. In the first half of the session, I do all the talking and make all my major predictions based on the information I pick up while holding onto an item of jewellery my client has provided. In the second half of the session, I invite my client to shuffle and then select a number of tarot cards. In every instance, the tarot cards chosen by the client mirror the predictions given in the first half of the session – further validating the predictions I made earlier.

Many people consult the tarot when they're

looking for direction, the best course of action to take, or predictions relating to their future.

Just recently, a prominent businessman consulted me. He asked, 'Do I take offer X or sell investment Y?' In his case, I invited him to shuffle the tarot while thinking about his two choices. Next, I asked him to focus on offer X and draw a card from the deck. Repeating the same procedure, he also drew a card for investment Y. When I turned the two cards over the stronger choice was immediate. While I was interpreting the meaning of the tarot cards he'd drawn, the businessman's spirit guide stepped in, adding to the validation. After I'd finished speaking, the businessman smiled and said, 'That's what my gut instinct was telling me.'

Crystal ball

I've lost count of the number of times I've rocked up for a radio interview or a guest appearance on a television show and someone has asked in jest, 'Where's your crystal ball?'

I feel sorry for the poor old crystal ball. It has borne the brunt of cartoons, jokes, and comedy sketches aimed at poking fun at psychics. Even so, many psychics still read using a crystal ball – and with good effect, I might add.

Some psychics cup the crystal ball in their hands and look down into it while others may rest the ball on a stand and peer into it. I know one psychic who cups the crystal ball in his hands and closes his eyes. He relies on psychic information travelling from the crystal ball through to his third eye. Another psychic I know says images float above the crystal ball like a three-dimensional movie.

In the past, I've used a crystal ball to jump-start my psychic intuition. I see beautiful light-filled stars and soft clouds of colour. My psychic impressions stem from the shape, colour, and patterns I see forming in the ball. For example, light green clouds may signify new beginnings or that money is forming on the horizon. A bright gold star, on the other hand, often signifies a departed loved one is providing a guiding light in my client's life.

Tea leaves

There is nothing more soothing than a relaxing cup of tea. Imagine combining that feeling with a psychic reading. That's exactly what psychic tea-leaf readers do. They offer a friendly and social experience with insights about your present and future.

Tea-leaf reading is an ancient form of divination. It has been around for centuries. And as I mentioned in chapter one, it's a subject close to my heart. I have so many fond memories of being taught tea-leaf reading by my Nanna.

While no two tea-leaf readers will ever conduct the exact same ritual, there are commonalities. Generally, you'll be asked to enjoy a cup of freshly brewed tea, leaving only half a teaspoon of liquid in the bottom of your cup. Some tea-leaf readers will ask you to swirl the tea leaves, stop, and then hand the cup to them.

The formation and position of the tea leaves are examined and interpreted based on the way they have formed on the inside of your cup.

My Nanna insists on using a loose broad-leaf tea. She believes the larger and varied tea-leaf shapes form clearer symbols. When I was young, I used to ask Nanna, 'What will today bring?' And she'd always reply, 'The answer is in your teacup.'

If you're a coffee drinker, don't despair. Divination with coffee followed tea-leaf reading. It's virtually the same process.

Psychometry

Psychometry is the art of holding a personal object – such as a watch, ring, or pendant – and gaining psychic impressions from the energy stored within it.

I prefer to start my readings with psychometry. It fast-tracks my connection with my client's energy. Within seconds of holding an object belonging to my client, I begin downloading psychic impressions relating to their past, present, and future. Psychometry also works in the same way for heirlooms and historic buildings. People often say, 'If only these walls could talk.' Well for psychics skilled in psychometry, like me, they can.

One of my most memorable psychometric readings was when I appeared on the television show *The One*. The producers asked us (the psychics) to select a piece of jewellery from a tray. Our job was to give a blind reading based on the information we obtained psychically from the piece of jewellery we selected. After which, we had to identify the rightful owner from within the audience. I chose a pendant suspended on a gold chain.

The physical characteristics of the owner came through instantly, as did information about her past, present, and future. But as I was performing the reading, a spirit voice broke through and took me by surprise. All I could hear was, 'That's mine.' This confused me because I knew the pendant did not belong to anyone in spirit. One person had only ever worn the pendant and she was still alive. Yet, this spirit was insistent the pendant belonged to her. In fact, she became so insistent she took over the entire reading. And when I'd finished I realised I'd spent most of the time describing her in intricate detail as if I were looking at a photograph. When the owner of the pendant stood up from among the audience members, she was amazed. My description of the insistent spirit coming through matched her departed mother perfectly.

What I didn't realise was that the pendant I was holding was a cleverly disguised locket. Nestled inside the locket was a photograph of the woman's dearly departed mother. When I heard, 'That's mine,' she was meaning, 'That's *my* photograph. Tell my daughter I know she put my photograph in her locket.'

The woman in the audience was overwhelmed with joy. I'd given her validation her mother knew about the locket.

Astrology

For centuries now, the stars and planets have inspired a sense of divine wonder in many. Astrology is the study of the patterns and relationships between the planets, sun, and moon in motion over time. Astrologers use this celestial clock to create horoscopes, birth charts, and give long-range forecasts.

To create an accurate astrological birth chart an astrologer will need to know the date, exact time, and place of your birth. From your chart, astrologers are able to offer you an insight into the intrinsic dimensions of your personality, your moods, your strengths and weaknesses through to long-range forecasts and the cosmic highlights of your life. Astrologers can also compare your birth chart with a love interest, family members, or siblings to find out the compatibility and longevity of your relationships.

Alongside the skill of astrology is numerology. By assessing your date of birth, a numerologist can find the ruling numbers that influence your personality, spiritual lesson, and life cycles as you fulfil your destiny.

Getting the most from your reading

A journalist once asked me, 'What is it like to raise the dead?' My reply was, 'I don't raise the dead. The client does.'

What many people don't realise is that I don't bring departed loved ones and spirit guides to a reading, the client does. Spirit chooses to come back and communicate because of the loving bond they share with their loved one. I merely bridge the communication gap between the physical and Spirit worlds.

That's why it is so important to prepare for your reading. Getting the best from your reading includes good preparation on your part.

The day before your appointment, review your list of questions. Make time to sit quietly.

Ask your loved ones and spirit guides to come in around you and be near. In your mind, run through the questions you'd like answered during your reading.

If your questions relate to a particular love interest, family member, child, or sibling find a suitable photograph of them. Some psychics will give you the opportunity to show photographs. Given I prefer only one person to feature in the photograph, I recommend making a photocopy and cutting out the person of interest. I also ask my clients to bring along a piece of jewellery worn solely by themselves or a departed loved one, depending on which reading they are having.

On the day of your appointment, arrive on time. Running ten minutes late may mean your session is cut short by ten minutes. Busy psychics often have bookings back to back. If so, it's not possible to extend your allotted time. So be on time to avoid disappointment.

Should you arrive early, sit quietly, and

wait. Close your eyes. Invite your departed loved ones and spirit guides to surround you in a loving protective gold light. Give them permission to come forward with messages and the answers to your questions. This will help you to focus and assist with opening up a connection with your loved ones in the Spirit World in preparation for your reading.

Before my client arrives for a reading, for example, I take a few moments to talk to my own spirit guides. I ask them to gather my client's departed loved ones and help guide them through. I also ask Spirit to deliver the best possible information for my client.

Sometimes prior to my client arriving for their session I find their departed loved ones arrive ahead of time and are close by, eager to pass on messages from the Spirit World. This often results in many happy reunions. But it's important to remember I don't have a psychic remote control. I can't channel-surf and select your favourite dearly departed. It's important to realise Spirit has a mission too. Even though you may desperately want your departed aunty to answer a question, she may not be the most qualified to do so. Trust that Spirit will answer most, if not all, of your questions. *Who* and *how* will be the surprise.

The best idea is to arrive at your reading with an open mind. Drop all expectations concerning Spirit or likely outcomes. Once you're seated in front of the psychic – wait for instructions. I always start with a rundown of the session – explaining I leave plenty of time for questions at the end.

It's normal to feel nervous before a reading – especially if it is your first. When you find yourself feeling a little tense or anxious take a few deep breaths and relax. In your mind, run through the questions you most want answered. You'll be amazed at how quickly the answers come through once the reading begins. Remaining open and relaxed during a reading will help the psychic amplify the connection with Spirit. Many wonderful things can happen in a reading when you relax. In the past, my clients have reported sensing their loved one in the room. Some have even sensed a kiss on the cheek or a soft touch on their hand.

At no time should a psychic pump you for additional information. To do so raises serious doubts as to the integrity of their psychic abilities.

The idea in any psychic session is to give minimal information and let the psychic do all the talking. Your part is to confirm or clarify the points made. For instance, I might say, 'I have a loved one here with an M name that sounds like Mark or Marcus.' You might respond with, 'I have an uncle who passed who we called Mark but Mum called him Marcus.' At that point, I'm likely to motion stop. Once you validate the information I receive from Spirit is correct I don't need further details. All professional psychic mediums work that way.

Total recall of the predictions, guidance, and

messages given during a reading days, weeks, or months later can be a challenge. For that reason, most psychics will offer to record your session in some way. If not, they usually invite you to bring your own recording device or welcome you to take notes. I offer my clients a variety of recording options – even a digital MP3 audio file. Avoid any psychic who refuses you the right to record or document your session.

With the advent of sophisticated web technology, online psychic chat services are becoming increasingly popular. If you feel compelled to engage such a service, the same principles apply. First, make sure the service is legitimate and professional. Unfortunately, a small number of unscrupulous operators are giving legitimate web chat services a bad name. Second, ensure you identify all charges before you proceed. Third, have your list of questions prepared. Remember most web-based psychic chat services charge by the minute.

Interpretation and timing

Never throw away your recorded readings or notes. Predictions don't always eventuate in the forecasted timeframe. This is because time has no relevance in the Spirit World. Time, as we understand it, only governs the physical world.

If I ask Spirit *when* an event is likely to occur for my client they answer with various combinations of symbols and sensations. For example, I might feel a cool breeze on my face to indicate winter. Other times a numeral could flash before my mind's eye. The challenge for me is to interpret what measurement of time the number or symbol represents. It could be hours, days, weeks, months, or years. Sometimes Spirit attempts to clarify time for me, but they don't always get it right.

I recall Regina, a client of mine. She and her husband were desperately trying to fall pregnant. When I asked Spirit *if* they would fall pregnant and *when*, Spirit delighted in showing me two beautiful blue butterflies. They were hovering above a tree filled with autumn leaves. I sensed Spirit was telling me Regina would fall pregnant naturally and I was given the numbers one or two to symbolise the timeframe. I felt sure she would give birth to a healthy baby boy – most likely in an autumn month. Of what year I was unsure. So you can imagine my surprise when I received a thank you card two years on from the reading. Enclosed in the card was a photograph of twin baby boys. Regina had fallen pregnant naturally and given birth to *two* baby boys in May (Autumn) two years after the reading.

So it pays to remind yourself that messages received from Spirit are filtered and interpreted using the psychic's personal knowledge base. What the psychic says and what you interpret those words to mean can be very different. In some ways, it's not unlike trying to describe an abstract painting to a friend over the phone. What you describe as alive and vibrant splashes of magnificent reds and oranges your friend may interpret as something that looks like a fierce fire.

Sandy, a client of mine, recalled a session she had with a clairvoyant many years ago. The clairvoyant was well into her sixties. When she said she could see Sandy working in a place with lots of television sets, Sandy was convinced her dream of working for a Hollywood movie studio was going to come true.

Twelve months later, Sandy was still working in Australia. Disillusioned, she changed jobs and took on a new role as a production manager for a computer games company. One day, while standing on the mezzanine floor looking down on all the computer programmers' workstations, Sandy realised the clairvoyant was right. She was surrounded by television sets – except they were computer monitors.

In any reading, there is room for interpretation. So it makes sense that a psychic's skills, level of maturity, and life experiences have an enormous impact on the information given in a reading. That's why I say readings should guide you, not rule you.

Just to add to the challenge of receiving, filtering, and interpreting messages, Spirit sometimes throws a curve ball from the world of opposites. Many psychics report numbers as mirror images. That's why I say things like, 'I'm seeing the number 12, but it could also represent 21.'

In my case, I know when I sense a pain on one side of my body, it relates to the opposite side of my client's body. My spirit guides joke with me and call it my 'psychic dyslexia'. But it's not exclusive to me. Many psychics worldwide report a similar psychic 'affliction'. You'll discover most psychics are aware when opposites are in play and they will inform you.

Just as psychics receive messages in different forms, they also sense Spirit in different ways. Some psychics see Spirit standing next to their client. For them, Spirit can appear as a solid form or a semitransparent shape – much like a hologram. Those who do not see, often feel and hear Spirit when they are close by, visiting the earth plane.

I feel privileged and humbled by my gift. I see, hear, and feel all aspects of Spirit. At times, my connections are so strong departed loved ones present to me ahead of their loved one's appointment.

This is especially so when I respond to letters and emails for *That's Life* magazine. As soon as the content of a particular letter sparks my interest, my connection with Spirit is instant. Like a flash, that reader's departed loved ones take advantage of the connection. Sometimes they'll pop in and out of my mind all day. As you can imagine, that can make things a little chaotic for me. But ultimately, it shows that our departed loved ones are willing to help and that they love and miss us.

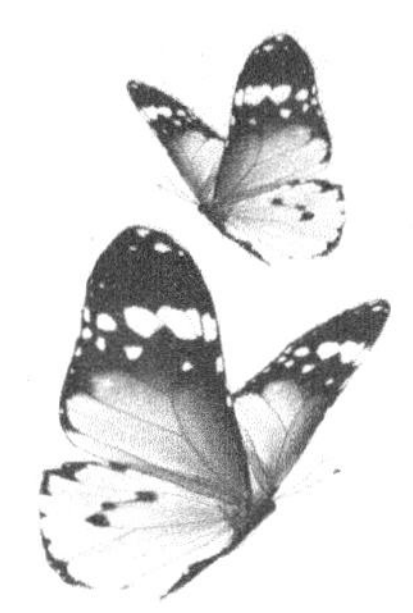

CHAPTER 11

MOST ASKED QUESTIONS

Do spirits eat?

Marcus, a seven-year-old boy, emailed this question to me. He'd recently lost his father. His mother had told him that even though his dad had gone to Heaven his spirit would live on. So each night Marcus left one biscuit and a glass of milk on a serving tray in the kitchen just in case there was no one to cook dinner for his dad.

Marcus's father came through the instant I read the email. His answer made me laugh. He asked me to tell Marcus that he could only eat the love Marcus sends. Biscuits fall straight through and down to his feet.

Do spirits watch us during our most intimate moments?

Spirits don't view your life as their own private reality show, so don't worry. Your intimate moments are private but your secrets may not be.

I remember Joan. She came to me for a reading. Joan's husband, Sid, was a newly diagnosed diabetic. Helping Sid reduce his daily intake of sugar was proving a struggle. Sid's dearly departed mother was the first one to jump through and insist I tell Joan where Sid was hiding a stash of chocolate.

Is it bad luck to buy your own tarot cards?

The idea that someone must give you your first deck of tarot cards or the deck brings bad luck – is a myth.

There are hundreds of tarot decks from which to choose. When purchasing tarot cards I recommend looking for two elements. First is the design. Choose artwork, colours, and symbolism that resonate with you. Second is the *feel*. Hold the tarot deck. Ask yourself, 'Do I like the energy coming from these cards? Do they feel *right*?' If you're a newcomer to tarot cards, keep an eye out for 'beginner' decks. You can always upgrade once you have a little more experience.

What is table-tipping?

Table-tipping is another way of communicating with the Spirit World. At the turn of the nineteenth century, it was very popular with members of the spiritualist movement.

Today, participants sit at a small lightweight table. They place their hands, palms down, on the tabletop and focus on raising their individual energy vibration. The medium leading the session combines the group's collective energy vibration with their psychic energy and uses it to call on the Spirit World.

In my experience, the table starts to vibrate, rattle, or shake with increasing intensity when Spirit is present in the room. At that point, the medium instructs Spirit how to communicate using the table. For example, the medium might say, 'Tip the table once to the left for yes and twice to the right for no.'

What is a ouija board and are they dangerous?

A ouija board is a board printed with the letters of the alphabet, numerals, and the words 'yes', 'no', and 'goodbye'. Participants rest their fingers on an indicator known as a *planchette*, which glides over the board to spell out messages from Beyond.

In the hands of novices, the ouija board can become a Pandora's box – and in some instances risks attracting low vibration souls that broadcast 'dark' energy. For that reason, I'm not a fan of the ouija board. It's not a toy; nor should it be used as a game to entertain guests!

How can I help my child develop psychic abilities?

If you believe your child has psychic ability, there are many excellent books specifically geared toward helping children develop their gift, which can give you more detailed advice.

I was fortunate that my mum understood the mystical ways of Spirit and encouraged the development of my gift. She would often impart wisdoms and share with me important spiritual values like, 'The universe will always provide,' and, 'Leave it to the capable hands of Spirit.'

You can help by making sure your child's psychic gifts develop in a positive, safe, empowering, and loving environment. Use techniques that foster a belief in the good of humankind, and deepen the communication and understanding between you and your child. Above all, the techniques must help your child navigate through what is an overwhelming journey, while still allowing them to be a child.

What is residual energy?

Residual energy is the term used to describe psychic energy stored within an object or place.

I have a friend who refuses to buy antique jewellery because of 'residual' energy. Her argument is that she doesn't want to risk tapping into the emotions and vibrations stored in the jewellery by previous owners.

I know others who are exactly the opposite. They purposely seek out 'haunted' buildings and visit old historical sites in the hope of seeing or sensing residual energy.

If your dominant psychic sense is *seeing* then you'll most likely find images from the past play out much like watching actors rehearsing a scene in a play. However, if your dominant psychic sense is *feeling* you're likely to experience residual emotions. And if your dominant psychic sense is *hearing* then noises, voices and sounds from the past may present like fragments of a radio play. Scream or faint, nothing you do will put the residual energy off its course of action. So if you do encounter such an energy, take a deep breath, and observe – then, if you feel compelled to, run!

Does my child have special needs because of bad karma?

A teacher once told a client of mine that her special needs son was born with his disability because he was paying for bad karma accumulated in a previous life. Not only is that a horrible, cruel, and judgmental thing to say, it is *false.* If anything, the opposite is true. Only an incredibly advanced soul would design a life as a special needs child. We should all look upon special needs children as brilliantly advanced souls who deserve our unconditional love and profound respect and support.

Does the Spirit World give out winning lottery numbers or tip-offs?

Rarely does a day go by where someone doesn't ask me to ask Spirit for the winning lottery numbers. Here's the thing. If winning the lottery is not written into your soul print – then it's unlikely that your numbers will be drawn. Tip-offs that prove lucky, on the other hand, are a different matter.

Once I was a celebrity guest at a gala event hosted by a well-known radio station. Every guest received a raffle ticket upon entry to win CDs and prizes. During the course of the evening, I found a ticket lying on the ground. I picked it up and handed it to the person nearest me. 'Hold onto this,' I said, 'you might just win.' She did. Spirit tipped me off – it was a lucky winning ticket.

Are you ever able to tune out from the Spirit World?

The short answer is no. In my life, Spirit World chatter is constant. It never stops. But what I can do is turn down the volume – just as you might do when the TV or radio interferes with your conversation or train of thought. However, I'm always listening out for interesting or important snippets of information. When I hear them I immediately turn up the volume.

Do animals and pets have a sixth sense?

Absolutely – animals do have a sixth sense. You only have to consider all the amazing animal survival stories recorded during times of natural disasters where hundreds of people were killed, yet most of the animals managed to find safety long before disaster struck.

Animals are very sensitive to energy vibrations. Pets in particular are extremely in tune with their owners. Any changes in mood, emotion, or wellbeing and much-loved pets are by their owners' side immediately.

I just love reading stories about farm dogs who know when it's time to take a two-kilometre trek down the driveway just so they can welcome the kids home as they step off the school bus.

Many dog owners attest to their dog's judge of character. I have one client who is a property manager. Her dog accompanies her to all potential new tenant interviews. If her dog rumbles a low-level growl during the interview, experience has taught her not to accept that person's rental application.

When dogs sense Spirit, they often bark and stare intensely at the one spot. There have even been reports of dogs behaving oddly in front of a photograph of a loved one passed. Cats often run laps around the house or meow incessantly for no obvious reason when Spirit is present. There have been reports of cats that suddenly start purring and padding down a departed loved one's chair as if the loved one was sitting in it.

Our pets are capable of hearing sounds and sensing natural and cosmic vibrations way beyond human capabilities. They are very much in tune with the celestial clock and Spirit World. So the next time you think your pet is behaving oddly or has gone completely mad, think again. Maybe you're receiving a call from the Afterlife.

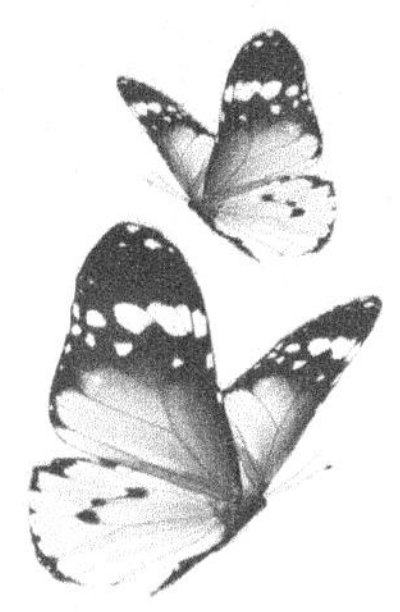

Afterword

As you continue along your spiritual path you may like to meditate upon the following wisdoms:

> Spirit teach me quiet – for it is in the stillness that I hear your voice.
>
> Spirit teach me courage – for there are times when I feel alone but I know I am not.
>
> Spirit teach me love – for there are times when I forget that I am a jewel in life's crown of unequalled beauty.

Love and guidance abounds in the Afterlife. For divine help all you need to do is ask – remember your departed loved ones are never too far away.

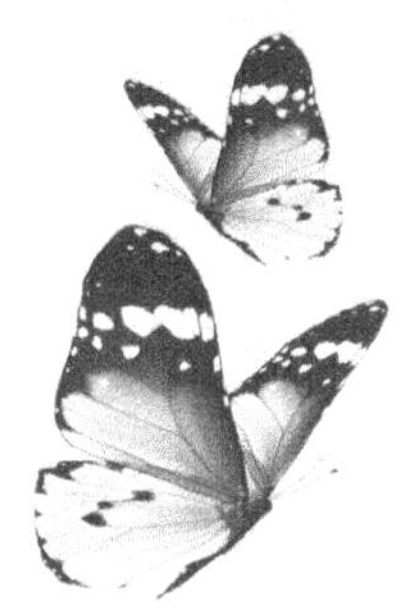

Acknowledgments

I truly humbled and blessed by the wealth of support, inspiration, and encouragement given to me by so many generous people along my spiritual path.

Especially:

My loving family Maria Coombes, Justin Coombes, and Lucia and Lino Marano whose unconditional love, support and encouragement of my spiritual gifts have touched my heart and enriched my soul.

Robert Reeves, whose love, kindness, and support is a priceless gift. You are the best angel on Earth I could ask for!

My dear loyal friends, too many to name. You are all tressures in my life. Thank you for always being there.

To my wonderful editor Denise Gibb, a true wordsmith and without whom this book would be so much less.

With special appreciation to the entire publishing team at Brio Books, for their continued enthusiasm, support, and for giving my books a new life.

With deep appreciation to those in the Spirit World and the wonderful people who've contributed their true-life stories to this book.

Last but by no means least, my spirit guide Red Feather, who has stood by my side and continues to be a guiding light in my life. Thank you for taking this journey with me.

With eternal gratitude, I thank you all from my heart.

— Mitchell Coombes

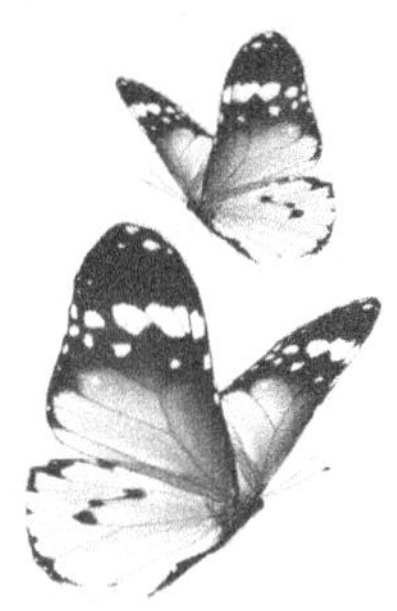

Bibliography

Books

Brown, Sylvia with Harrison, Lindsay. *Psychic Children: revealing the intuitive gifts and hidden abilities of boys and girls*, Piatkus, Great Britian, 2009.

Brown, Sylvia with Harrison, Lindsay. *The Other Side and back: a psychic's guide to our world and beyond*, New American Library, New York, 2002.

Dent, Margaret. *Love never dies: extraordinary accounts of survival beyond death*, Random House, Australia, 1999.

Edward, John. *Infinite Quest: develop your psychic intuition to take charge of your life*, Stirling Publishing, New York, 2010.

Eddy, Steve. *Timeless wisdom of the Native Americans: a beginner's guide*, Hodder & Stoughton, London, 2000.

Hardo, Trutz. *Children Who Have Lived Before: Children from all over the world prove that they have lived before*, Rider, London, 2005.

Melody. *Love is in the Earth: A Kaleidoscope of Crystals*

(updated), Earth-Love Publishing House, Colorado, 2005.

Myss, Caroline. *Sacred Contracts: awakening your divine potential*, Bantam Books, Sydney, 2001.

Rogers, Rita. *Mysteries: first-hand accounts of the amazing world of the unexplained*, Pan Macmillan, London, 2001.

Van Praagh, James. *Ghosts Among Us: uncovering the truth about the Other Side*, Rider, London, 2009.

Van Praagh, *James. Heaven and Earth: making the psychic connection*, Ryder Books, London, 2003.

Van Praagh, James. *Healing Grief: reclaiming life after any loss*, Hodder Headline, Australia, 2004.

Van Praagh, James. *Talking to Heaven: a medium's message of life after death*, Penguin, New York, 1999.

Weiss, Brian L. *Many Lives Many Master: the true story of a prominent psychiatrist, his young patient and the past-life therapy that changed both their lives*, Piatkus, Great Britian, 2006.

Magazines

Coombes, Mitchell. *Cleanse the negative: the art of protection against psychic attack, Insight Magazine*, April 2006, page 50, Insight Publishing Pty Ltd.

Bibliography

Websites

American Association of Electronic Voice Phenomena. **www.aaevp.com** (NB: This redirects to a different page: www.atransc.org/)

Anadi Teaching. *The teaching of enlightenment: the blueprint of the soul,* 2008 **www.anaditeaching.com/teachingsoul4.htm**

BBC Religion. *The Dalai Lama: role of the Dalai Lama,* 21/09/2006. **www.bbc.co.uk/religion/religions/buddhism/people/dalailama_1.shtml**

Mott, Maryanne. Did Animals Sense Tsunami Was Coming? National Geographic, 4 January 2005. **www.news.nationalgeographic.com/news/2005/01/0104_050104_tsunami_animals.html**

Near-Death experiences and the Afterlife. *Dr. Ian Stevenson: The Pioneer of Reincarnation Research*, 2008. **www.near-death.com/experiences/reincarnation01.html**

Stillpoint Communications Inc. *Jerry Thomas. Blueprint of the Soul.* **www.greatpeace.net**

Wytchyways. *New Idea, Out of This World. Protect Yourself*, page 83. **www.wytchyways.com/serene_psychic.pdf**

Also available by Mitchell Coombes

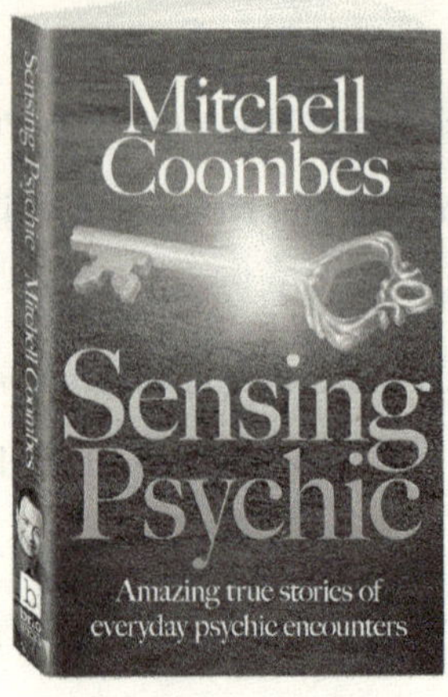

Have you ever had a psychic dream or compelling feeling? Does an inner voice guide the decisions you make? Can our pets really be spiritual messengers? Is it true all children are born psychic?

Drawing on his remarkable life and years of experience, celebrity medium Mitchell Coombes explains how people from all walks of life experience incredible moments of psychic awakening that defy logic. Astonished parents talk about the amazing intuitive gifts of their young children. Pet lovers recall heart-breaking moments of saying goodbye to a much-loved pet – only to sense their welcome return from the Spirit World, days, months, or even years later. Packed with profound, life-changing psychic encounters, Mitchell also reveals simple ways of 'tuning in' to receive intuitive guidance. *Sensing Psychic* will give you the keys to open the doors for your very own psychic journey.

9781922598738 (print)
9781925143065 (eBook)

Also available by Mitchell Coombes

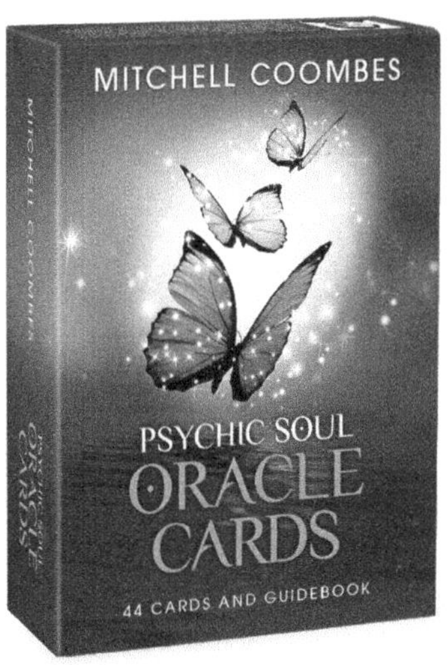

The Psychic Soul Oracle Cards by spiritual medium and bestselling author, Mitchell Coombes, offer divine guidance and answers to questions about your love life, career, health, spiritual path and more.

Each of the 44 oracle cards in this unique deck features a beautiful crystal butterfly to help you tune into your intuition and awaken your psychic senses.

With the help of the accompanying guidebook, you'll discover the meaning of each card, the healing qualities of each crystal, and learn how to easily give yourself and others accurate and insightful readings.

9781925143072 (print)